Recent Research in Psychology

Ingrid Pramling

Learning to Learn

A Study of Swedish Preschool Children

Springer-Verlag
New York Berlin Heidelberg
London Paris Tokyo Hong Kong

Ingrid Pramling
Institutionen för Padagogik
Göteborgs Universitet
S-43126 Mölndal
Sweden

Library of Congress Cataloging-in-Publication Data
Pramling, Ingrid.
    [Att lära barn lära.   English]
    Learning to learn: a study of Swedish preschool children/Ingrid
Pramling.
       p.   cm.—(Recent research in psychology)
    Translation of: Att lära barn lära.
    Includes bibliographical references.
    ISBN 0-387-97122-X (alk. paper)
    1. Learning.   2. Cognition in children.   3. Preschool children—
Sweden—Case studies.   I. Title.   II. Series.
LB1060.P6913   1990
370.15'23—dc20   89-37723

Printed on acid-free paper.

Camera-ready copy prepared by the author.
Printed and bound by Edwards Brothers, Inc., Ann Arbor, Michigan.
Printed in the United States of America.

9 8 7 6 5 4 3 2 1

ISBN 0-387-97122-X Springer-Verlag New York Berlin Heidelberg
ISBN 3-540-97122-X Springer-Verlag Berlin Heidelberg New York

Foreword

For eight years, since I began my research, my main concern has been to understand children and their world. The first step towards understanding how children think was taken in connection with my thesis, which I presented five years ago. This was a description of how children in the age group three to eight years conceive their own learning. The thesis was published in the same series as the present monograph and is entitled "The child's conception of learning". The main emphasis in this study was on developmental psychology.

As I have worked as a preschool teacher myself, I am extremely anxious that my research will be of benefit to my former colleagues. I have therefore devoted a great deal of time to writing and collaborating in numerous books of popular science. These have always been based on my own research. Now, however, the time is ripe for taking a new step, based on new research, towards understanding children and helping others to understand them., this time by publishing "Learning to learn", which is a description of how children have actually been taught to learn in preschool. In this type of study it is not a question of first obtaining results of the nature of basic research and then applying them in the educational setting, but both aspects are integrated in that the starting-point is the phenomena that are of importance to children in their everyday life.

A number of people have supported and assisted me in my work. Professor Ference Marton, my supervisor when I was a doctoral student, has continued to be an enthusiastic colleague, who has always been willing to discuss research and who has read my manuscript and given me invaluable advice.

One important resource in my work has been to have "neighbours and colleagues" like Jan Erik Johansson, Claes-Göran Wenestam and Maj

Asplund Carlsson, with whom I have been able discuss most things over a cup of coffee. Margareta Sjökvist typed out all the original interviews with the children, Karin Klingenstjärna read the proofs and Lars Gunnarsson and Åsa Berntsson were responsible for the final editing.

Other persons who have been of great help are Elisabet Doverborg, who worked very hard in her capacity of co-judge, Vivianne Andersson, who has carried out some of the learning experiments, and, of course, the four preschool teachers and their children who so generously shared their thoughts and experience and without whose help this study could not have been implemented. I would also like to mention the Natural History Museum in Gothenburg, which collaborated in one of the experiments.

The project on which this monograph is based was carried out with funds from the Swedish Council for Research in the Humanities and Social Sciences. I am also grateful for having received travel grants, enabling me to make contacts with colleagues in other countries, from the Department of Education, Wilhelm and Martina Lundgren's fund, Knut and Alice Wallenberg's fund, Gunnel Carlsson's fund, the Royal Academy of Arts and Sciences in Gothenburg and the Adlerbert research fund.

Finally, thanks to my family, Kalle, Tommy and Niklas for support and encouragement.

Mölndal September 1988

Ingrid Pramling

Translated into English by Gillian Thylander

CONTENTS

PART 4 DISCUSSION

Abstract

The present study is based on previous research into children's conceptions of learning, which were traced and described in terms of qualitatively different forms of thinking about what they learnt and how learning came about. Another earlier study was devoted to discovering ways of influencing the children's conceptions of their own learning, and positive results were obtained.

The purpose of the present study has been to find out if children can learn better (in a qualitatively different way) after being involved in a programme with a specific didactic approach than children involved in more common preschool programs do. The assumptions are that learning is a question of taking the children's perspective and of focusing on developing their conceptions of the various phenomena that are brought up for discussion throughout the preschool year.

The specifc didactic approach is based on using everyday situations, created by the children or the teacher, and reflecting on them in ways expected to develop the children's conceptions. The children's reflections were encouraged on three levels of generality: about the content, about the structure of the content (many types of "content" or themes have a common basic structure, which has to be conceptualised in order to understand the phenomena), and about their own learning. The didactic approach may be described in terms of a vertical variation in the level of thinking. It is a vertical alternation between the specific and the more general and vice versa. Metacognition is focused on at each of the three levels, that is, how they think about the content, the structure and their learning of the content.

This "descriptive-experimental" study comprised four groups of preschool children (in total 76 children between 5 and 6 years of age), with their teachers. Two of the groups, A and B, were experimental, that is, they worked in accordance with the purpose of the study and two, C and D, served as control groups.

The method of the study is based on qualitative analysis of clinical interviews (similar to the Piagetian ones), where the purpose is to find similarities and differences in children's under-standing of the phenomena discussed.The childrens' conceptions of learning that were identified from interviews at the beginning of the year were the basic starting point. At the end of the year all groups participated in three learning experiments, involving a story or a lesson and followed by interviews, to see what development, measured in relation to qualitative changes in children's thinking and understanding, had taken place.

The results show that the children in the experimental group not only developed their conceptions of learning to a large extent, but also understood the meaning of the messages conveyed in the learning experiments in a better way. The differences are outstanding between the experimental and control groups. In other words, children involved in the specific didactic approach adopted here developed the skill to learn.

Keywords: Developmentalpsychology, learning, metacognition, phenomenography, preschool, qualitative research.

1. INTRODUCTION

This publication deals with the main study within the project "Meta-learning in the preschool" carried out in the period 1985-1988 with economic support from The Swedish Council for Research in the Humanities and Social Sciences (HSFR). The other studies in the project have been presented in reports and papers. The report "Meta-inlärning i förskolan. En fenomenografisk studie" (Meta-learning in the preschool. A phenomenographic study) (Pramling, 1987c) describes the design and implementation of the main study, so that there is some overlapping in this publication with regard to these aspects. The empirical material on which the present study is based was collected during the academic year 1986-1987.

The theoretical starting-point is phenomenographic, that is, the research approach adopted in this work is that of distinguishing and describing people's conceptions of various phenomena in the world around them (Marton, 1981).

Two main types of aspects have been considered during the work. Those of developmental psychology consist in descriptions of variations in ways of thinking, including possible variations in the course of time. Those of learning psychology are based on a hypothesis that the reflections of children lead to development, and that the more children are aware of their own learning, the "better" they are at learning.

The project is in the nature of basic research but its implications may be within the sphere of both general didactics and preschool didactics. The general didactic implications are that a teacher benefits from knowing about the different ways children think. Knowing what form a sequence of children's spontaneous ideas can take helps the teacher both to discover how children think and provides the necessary conditions for developing the children's ideas towards new insight. Another aspect is that the teacher can avail him/herself of children's ideas in an educational context, that is, by releasing the wealth of ideas. Focusing on them in all their variety makes these ideas stand out as examples of different ways of thinking (Lybeck, 1981). The preschool didactic*_ implications are that goals must be set in relation to an educational purpose, that is, the particular kinds of insight one wishes to develop in the children. (* Preschool in Sweden is for children up to 7 years of age, while they start primary school at 7.)

We have applied our knowledge of how children think about a certain theme and deliberately tried to develop their insight in relation to the content in the theme "The shop". This theme has been studied and evaluated within the framework of the main study, but has been reported in another connection (Pramling, 1988), so that it will not be dealt with here in any detail.

The origin of the study reported here is to be found within phenomenography, in a survey of children's conceptions of their own learning (Pramling, 1983a). In this the children's qualitatively different ways of thinking about learning were described as a question of what and how they learn. The children's statements were interpreted as expressing different levels of metacognitive awareness, in the same way as children's messages are interpreted in the area of meta-communication as expressing something beyond the words themselves (Hamilton, 1986). Several different approaches are adopted within the field of metacognitive research (see Pramling, 1987b). The metacognitive hypothesis used in Pramling (1983a) is that that metacognition is a question of how children think about their own learning.

The next step leading up to the present work is a study within the framework of the project dealing with how children's conceptions of learning can be developed by using their own thoughts and reflections on learning (Pramling, 1986b; Pramling, 1988b).

The third step, which this main study will investigate, is whether and in what way metacognition is expressed in cognition, that is, whether children learn "better" or qualitatively different things if they are more aware of their own learning. The question the project is attempting to answer is: Can a teacher help to improve children's learning by systematically applying a special didactic idea?

One works with developing children's understanding by letting them reflect on certain specific <u>contents</u> connected with understanding, about the <u>structure</u> of the contents (in order to understand relationships) and about their own <u>learning</u>. Within all three levels the teacher also directs the children's thoughts towards a metacognitive level by getting them to reflect on how they themselves and others think about the content, structure and learning. In other words, it is a question of making the children aware of a vertical variation, that is, different levels of generality. There are many more levels of generality to be sure, but these have been reduced to three to make the way of working easier to grasp.

Two of the four preschools studied have endeavoured to apply the way of working briefly described above, which is expected to lead to an improvement in the children's learning. The other two preshool groups functioned as control groups. All the preschool children (totalling 76) were observed for one school year (which is divided into two terms only in Sweden, autumn and spring) and participated both in three learning experiments during the latter part of the spring term and in two interviews, one before and one after the experiments, about their conceptions of their own learning.

According to Kroksmark (1987), the ideas on which this type of didactic approach is based may be traced to Comenius, whom many consider to be the founder of modern didactics. Comenius regarded the "what" and "how" questions as inseparable. According to Kroksmark, it was Herbart's ideas that later led to the two different directions in didactics. One focused on the "what" questions and became more concerned with the theory related to the syllabus, the other focused on the "how" questions and thus became more concerned with teaching methods. The third question within didactics, "why", is one of evaluation and is not treated to the same extent.

A teacher must reach a decision on the basic questions of didactics - "what", "how" and "why" - whenever he/she selects a new content to work with. In this study, the "what" question implies developing children's capacity to learn in the sense to understand. The "how" question is answered by the way of working mentioned earlier. The "why" question is an evaluation of the hypothesis that it is more important for children to learn to learn (Rasmussen, 1988) than to learn a specific content. This applies even if learning to learn takes place in relation to specific contents. In the next stage a teacher can consider why these particular contents are selected.

This book contains the following parts: one on the background and dealing with views and points of departure, one on the research I have conducted myself, which forms the basis of this study. The part on methods contains a description of the design and implementation. It also contains a description of how the work was planned during the year and what tools were used. The third part deals with the results, both in the form of qualitative descriptions of children's conceptions and quantitative estimates of their frequency. In the final section, the significance and implications of the results regarding the content and way of working in the preschool are discussed.

PART 1. BACKGROUND

2. GENERAL THEORETICAL STARTING-POINTS

Marton (1988) distinguishes three types of competence which may form educational goals, namely, skills, knowledge and understanding. Skills refer to the way we <u>do</u> things and knowledge to what we <u>know</u> about phenomena that have already been discerned and conceived in some way. Understanding, on the other hand, refers to the way in which the phenomenon is discerned or <u>conceived</u> by the child.

Let us take the traffic theme in preschool as an example. Teaching children skills here involves teaching them to move about safely in the immediate environment simply by practising. To teach children facts about traffic implies that you teach them what various road signs mean, the difference between right and left, where to cross the street, relevant concepts, etc., by giving them information about these things. Teaching children to understand traffic means teaching them to discern and form an idea of traffic as traffic, that is, a mobile system with certain rules.

What children do in traffic or what they know about it is explained by other researchers on the basis of the "mental apparatus" that is assumed to be an inherent capacity of children, while perceiving traffic as a mobile system can be explained by the things in the world appearing to the child in a certain way. Marton (op cit) thinks that understanding cannot be described separately from the phenomenon that is understood. Nor can a phenomenon be described without describing the act of understanding itself. He holds that these two aspects do not even exist separately even if we talk about them as if they did. To understand the world around us as a form of experience has a relational character. A relationship always exists between individual understanding and the phenomenon one has understood. This means that one can choose to express either the perspective of the individual or that of the phenomenon. People understand or see a phenomenon in different ways, but we can also say that the phenomenon appears to people in different ways.

Much of Piaget's early research was concerned with taking the perspective of children and seeing how the same thing appeared in different ways to them (see, for example, Piaget, 1975; 1970; 1978). It is this particular aspect that phenomenography has adhered to. Frank Murray (NERA 1987), in his lecture on the subject, pointed out the three different directions Neo-Piagetian research has taken:

1. Determinations of the content of children's conceptual development.

2. Replications or extensions of the Piagetian empirical results regarding imitation, the permanence of objects, egocentricism, improvement of memory, conservation training, formal operations, etc.

3. Theoretical models concerning problems within "horisontal décalage", language, the formal characteristics of logical models, grouping of models in the concrete period, transfer mechanisms, etc.

None of these three directions can be attributed to phenomenograpy, which should be seen as research devoted to discerning how people understand the various phenomena in the world around them, even though both Murray and others who are researching into the conceptual development of children would perhaps regard these directions as comparable. The emphasis within phenomenography is not on what concepts children develop or do not develop, but on how they understand the concepts, problems, phenomena, situations, etc. they are confronted with.

An example of a child study based on the phenomenographic approach is that of Dahlgren and Olsson (1985) about reading from the point of view of children, that is, what conception preschool and primary school children have of reading and how it is done. Francis (1982) has carried out some interesting case studies to see how children enter into the language of reading and writing. She analyses children's understanding of their experience with regard to reading and writing and also the development of their knowledge of spelling during their first time at school. Francis analyses the children's progress or failure in relation to their experience of classroom activities, the reading method used by the teacher and home influences. Moreover, she clearly shows that it is impossible to make any generalisations about how the teaching method and background factors can affect children's reading.

Neuman (1987) has studied how children have spontaneously formed an idea of the numbers 1 - 10 when they begin in the first form. The children were given various problems to solve, for example, "I have two boxes and I'm thinking of hiding these 9 buttons in them. You can have five guesses how many I put in each box". By continually asking the children how they thought things out when they did something in one way or another, she elicited different conceptions of number and counting. It was shown that children who find arithmetic difficult actually <u>count,</u> in contrast to the successful ones who, according to Neuman, <u>see numerical structures</u> that help them to solve the problems. Doverborg (1987) has studied preschool children in a similar way. One question she asked was: "I have 5 (or 9) buttons here. Now I'm putting 6 (3 etc.) in one of these boxes. How many have I left to put in the other box then?" Doverborg finds that preschool children have already developed various kinds of strategies for solving this problem. She has also shown how children understand the phenomenon "to divide" as sharing equally, which implies that uneven numbers cannot be divided (see also Doverborg & Pramling, 1987).

As we have seen earlier, Marton (1988) argues that our understanding (conception) of the world is represented by a kind of competence that is distinct from and more fundamental than the other two forms of competence (skills and knowledge). If this is the case, it is reasonable to assume that the teacher should focus on this as a basis on which to develop the other types of competence. Smith (1986) is another researcher who argues that understanding precedes the learning of facts, but he also points out that most teaching is planned according to the opposite view, consisting as it does of loose parts without any connection and without any meaning to the child.

Taking the type of phenomenographic studies briefly described above as a starting-point, the implications are that work in preschool should concern children's conceptions of various phenomena as a basis of subsequent acquisition of knowledge in school. Accordingly, teaching children to learn is largely a matter of working with a base that is usually "invisible" (Pramling, 1987a). Marton (op cit) claims that a form of teaching in which the teacher finds out how children think in order to use this insight as a basis for developing a form of teaching whose object is the conception of phenomena is rare.

2.1 Metacognition

What then does the view developed here about children's cognition involve if it is to be applied at the metacognitive level?

Children's thoughts about their various cognitive processes, such as remembering, learning, understanding, solving problems, etc., are usually regarded as metacognitive aspects of thinking. Metacognitive research has attracted increasing attention in recent years, since it is assumed that children's metacognitive knowledge and skills play a decisive role in their ability to learn.

Three different approaches to metacognition can be distinguished. Flavell (1979) can be seen as representing one approach and as the one who has been at the forefront of development. He regards metacognition as a question of children's <u>knowledge of their own cognition</u>. that is, what children <u>know</u> about cognition. The empirical studies that can be attributed to this line of approach have nearly always been carried out in experimental situations. Moreover, the studies have largely concerned children of preschool and early school age. The framework of interpretation consists of general stages, often those of Piaget, unconnected with any particular content or situation. The research interest here is completely focused on developmental psychology without any educational implications. The conclusion that can be drawn is that children should not be taught anything that they are not ready for.

The second approach in metacognitive research concerns the <u>control and regulation of a person's cognition</u>. Brown (1985) can be regarded as the leading researcher in this area. Most empirical studies using this approach have been carried out in connection with education. Attempts have been made to find out what type of actions "clever" pupils perform and then to teach children these strategies. The studies are often based on learning something by reading texts. Consequently, the study subjects are schoolchildren, never preschool children. The framework of interpretation that forms the starting-point is information processing, based on the idea that there is a central control system in the brain whose function is to superintend and point out the direction when problems are to be solved (Brown & Reeve, 1985). This approach also appears to be unconnected with the content or the situation. The educational implications can therefore be seen as a question of teaching children strategies for learning. In other words, this approach is concerned with what children <u>do</u> in the learning situation.

The third approach is based on <u>the children's point of view</u> and regards qualitatively different categories of <u>conceptions as metacognition</u>, that is, how children understand. The framework of interpretation is a question of what appears in children's thinking about something in the world around them. Thus, this approach depends both on the content and the situation. Within the area of metacommunication, this way of interpreting children's statements, linked up with the idea that the child communicates its conception of something, is common. Bae (1988) describes a situation in which five-year-old Tom places two carrots (a fat one and a thin one) side by side when wanting to chop them up for vegetable soup. The child looks at his nursery school teacher and declares with satisfaction that he can chop them both at the same time. If you listen to what Tom is trying to communicate, says Bae, it is obvious that he has understood that you are cleverer and better if you can manage to chop up two carrots at the same time. In the metacommunicative perspective, it is often a question of the child expressing a conception of itself, while in the metacognitive perspective advocated here it is a question of looking at children's statements about various phenomena as an expression of their conception of the world around them.

To sum up, it may be said that the three different metacognitive approaches are based on different assumptions about the child as a cognitive being, which means that this phenomenon is studied by different methods. The educational implications also vary. Both the approach that emphasises children's knowledge and that which emphasises control and regulation are based on the assumption that children have a cognitive "apparatus" that is separate from the world, that is, they start off from a dualistic view of children's thinking. The third approach, which emphasises that the child has a conception of something, is based on the relation between children and the world, that is, children's thinking cannot be separated from the world since thinking is always directed towards something (Pramling, 1987d). This is an assumption that has its origin in the school of phenomenology (Merleau -

Ponty, 1962). As far as metacognition as knowledge or skill is concerned, it is seen as a question of whether the child has developed this or not, while in the case of metacognition as conceptions, the latter are always there although differing qualitatively from one individual to another. They do not only differ from one individual to another, but also within one and the same individual, depending on the content they are pondering over (Doverborg, Pramling & Qvarsell, 1987).

2.2 Children's conceptions of learning

2.2.1 A survey

The author (Pramling 1983a) has studied children's conceptions of learning previously. That study, based on developmental psychology, was concerned with investigating and describing the qualitatively different ways in which children think of their own learning. The results were described in terms of what children think they have learnt and how they think this has come about. When beginning to be aware of their own learning, children appear to have the idea that they learn something by doing something (a skill, activity or some form of behaviour).The next stage of development appears to be that children perceive that they can learn to know something (they talk about facts or knowledge as an intellectual ability). Finally, a conception of learning as understanding something appears (they see that something has come to have another meaning to them, possibly as a result of relating things to each other and drawing conclusions). The above-mentioned ways of thinking about learning that children express may be compared with the three views of learning that, according to Marton (1988), exist within learning research.

When it is a question, then, of how children think learning comes about, one can find a stage where they have not yet distinguished between doing and learning to do. The next stage in their awareness is connected with their seeing learning as a result of growing older. Finally, children realise that they learn through experience. However, even in this last conception, different ways of thinking can be found. When, for example, children perceive that they learn to do something by gaining experience, they express different kinds of experience. Some children only appear to perceive that they have learnt as a result of some action or activity they have been involved in. This conception involves the passage of time, that is, you have to go on doing something for a long time before you learn to do it. Other children have the idea that they can influence their learning themselves by, for example, interfering with the passage of time by practising harder in order to learn something.

The majority of four-year-olds already have the idea that you learn to do something by gaining experience in the form of your own actions. Some preschool children also spontaneously grasp the idea that you learn to know something by experience. But instead of having any conception of their own active experience, they connect knowledge and knowing with some adult telling them something while they themselves are passive consumers (Pramling, 1986a, 1988). The preschool child is, in other words, already on the way towards the traditional view of learning in school - acquiring knowledge by listening to the teacher. This is the case despite the fact that preschools have another philosophy and view of children than schools do and despite the fact that the teacher usually structures children's learning in themes, in which many different activities are included and integrated into a whole according to the teacher's viewpoint. Consequently, children see learning to know as a question of external influence (communication of other people's experience), while they more often regard learning to do things as a question of personal experience.

Various studies (Pramling, 1983a; 1986b) have also shown that teachers take various things in their classes for granted, something they should not do as it turns out. For example, teachers often assume that if you repeat the same things on different occasions they form parts of a connected sequence, that is, that you are training the same skill even though it is spread out in time. However, the difference between not being able to do something and being able to do it is perceived by younger children as a sudden change. When, instead, children become aware of a gradual change, an important step in their way of thinking has been taken. Eventually, children discover that they can learn something better. Being better may then mean both increasing one's competence qualitatively and developing it quantitively, that is, you not only learn "more", but you learn qualitatively different things. About 40% of the six-year-olds express that they perceive that they have improved their competence in some area, that is, a qualitative or a quantitative change has taken place. By the time the children are eight years of age the frequency of this conception has risen to about 75%. The idea of "being better" is based on a conception of continuity, which has a strong bearing on understanding that one learns and can influence one's own learning. Continuity means that children can preserve an identity in what they are learning and that they perceive a gradual change. It is necessary for an identity to be preserved in order that children should realise that it is the same learning process they are involved in, even if it is spread out in time. Gradual change means that, little by little, you become better at the thing you are learning, that is, your capacity increases. This means that when the child can identify different events over time as components of the same phenomenon (learning something), it can also perceive a gradual improvement.

As an example of this phenomenon, let us imagine that the child has to learn a telephone number. If you repeat a certain telephone number several times a day, these practice sessions are, from the adult point of view, parts of a whole, that is, they will eventually get to know the telephone number by heart. From the child's point of view, it is not at all obvious that these sessions are connected. To say one's telephone number one day need not, so to speak, have anything to do with saying it the next. For a child to integrate these events, he must have the idea that you learn by repetition.

2.2.2 Teaching in preschool

It is customary in preschools to organise children's learning in the form of themes (Doverborg & Pramling, 1988). This may mean, for example, that the area "The farm" is illustrated in many different ways: by the teacher talking about it, by her reading stories, through songs, by paying a visit to a farm, by enacting scenes, through creative activities, etc. To be able to understand that all these parts form a whole (the farm), children must be able to realise that different events can be part of the same process. That children do not see the visit to the riding school or making horses out of wood as anything but forms of amusement (Pramling, 1986a) thus stems from their way of thinking and perhaps also from the teacher's failure to make the learning structure clear to the children, just because she takes it for granted. The teacher often assumes that practical actions lead to insight. This is shown not least in her letting the children make a clock when her purpose is to teach children to tell the time. From the children's viewpoint, however, what they see as the thing they have learnt is the actual making of the clock. All the obvious assumptions that teacher has about something are never made the subject of reflection on the part of the children and can therefore limit their possibility of understanding. If children have not developed the conceptions on which the teaching is based, they run the risk of encountering learning problems later on, since the most fundamental concepts and types of insight have never been established (see, for example, Neuman, 1987).

Earlier studies (Pramling, 1983a) have shown that children find it difficult to connect what they learn in preschool with anything outside it. When, for example, they worked with the theme about "Forms", only a few children understood that forms were something concrete that existed outside preschool. As far as most children were concerned, forms remained just the four basic shapes the teacher had tried to teach them to remember the names of. In contrast, the theme of "The shop", studied later (Pramling, 1986b), was very much connected with real life. However, all themes are naturally not of this type, but it is the teacher's task to bring out this relationship, something thematisation itself is assumed to contribute to.

Focusing on the relation between the learning situation and real life can be a question of problematising and lifting up the concrete onto a more general plane, by, for example, make children aware of the principles of traffic when they are making road signs. But it can also be the opposite, to concretise and problematise more general and abstract things, by, for example, making the children aware of forms in real life when they are learning to distinguish one kind of form from another. Thematisation can work both ways, so to speak, depending on the subject concerned. However, it is necessary to focus on the relation between learning and the world around us, that is, get the children to understand that what they do here and now in preschool has something to do with real life outside it. Qvarsell (1988) has shown that, as they grow older, children in school make a more and more obvious distinction between what takes place in lessons and what happens outside. In view of this, it is even more important to get children to understand that it is the "world" they are learning about in preschool and school, not least because these activities should appear meaningful to them.

If we return to the theme about different forms, this is an example of a theme where abstract concepts such as square, rectangle, triangle and circle are dealt with. To focus on the relation between learning children to name and define different shapes and reality should consist in helping them to discover those forms that have some importance and meaning in everyday life. The traffic theme is an example of an activity where the opposite kind of strategy is needed, that is, lifting up the concrete on to a more general plane (Pramling, 1986b). The children made traffic signs, and they came to think of these as the main point of the traffic theme. What the teacher would need to do here is to point out the principles and the more abstract phenomena so that children would understand the relation to the world around them.

2.2.3 Developing children's conceptions

In a pilot study (Pramling, 1986b) one teacher worked with developing children's conceptions of learning by thematising and problematising the learning aspect under the theme The Shop. Two control groups worked with the same theme but without discussing anything at a metacognitive level. In comparison with the children in the other groups, the children in the experimental group developed their conceptions considerably both with regard to <u>what</u> they learned while working with the theme and <u>how</u> learning came about.They learned about their own learning through the teacher getting them to think about and reflect on what they were doing and how and why they were doing it.Their attention was also drawn to the fact that they thought about the various things they were working with in many different ways.

The time when the children were supposed to bake a cake is an example of this. Instead of taking out a recipe and starting off with this, the teacher creates a problem and asks the children how they should go about baking a cake. The children have to suggest different ingredients. "But how do we know how much to to take of each kind?" One child suggests that there are recipes. "But could we bake a cake without having a recipe?" teacher asks. Some children think you couldn't, while others believe you could. Other questions they have to ponder over are "How did people get the idea of writing down a recipe? Where has it come from?" All the different ideas the children are brought out and they teacher draws their attention to their variety. "Shall we go on experimenting until it tastes good, as Ollie suggests or can we break up a cake to see what it is made of, as Stina says?" The children decide to go by the taste. "But if the cake turns out to be really good, how could be bake one like it the next day?" "Tasting again," says one. "Is there any other way?" "If we want Mummy to bake it at home on Saturday, what should we do then?" Eventually the conversation comes round to the need to write down what they put in and to invent their own recipe! While the children are enjoying their cake the teacher raises the question: "Are there any other things we can find out by trial and error and by writing down what we have done?" The children's suggestions are noted down and tested out one by one. Constantly they were asked, "What did we find out by doing this?"

Another example refers to when the children are to visit the shop. Each of them then has to think out what they want to find out in the shop. They are urged to remember and find out what they have wondered about. On their return they have to talk about the answers they have found. "But how did get to know it was like that?" or "How did you find that out?" asks the teacher over and over again. "Just listen to how many different ways you have gone about finding out what you wondered about," she says. In other words, starting off from the content, the teacher directs the children's attention towards how they have got to know something, that is, learning.

The results of this pilot study show that it is possible to develop children's conceptions both of what they learn and of how this comes about. The learning aspect is brought out in the everyday situation and by "forcing" the children to think and reflect. While only a few children in the two normal preschools developed their conceptions of what they had learnt in preschool from learning to do to learning to know something, as many as three-quarters of the children in the experimental group did so. There is also an obvious difference between the experimental and the two control groups with regard to children's conceptions of how knowledge is acquired. More than half the children in the experimental group expressed that they had perceived that they were able to acquire knowledge through experience in the world around them, while the children in the other groups who had any idea at all said that they could get to know something by someone telling them about it. Thus, the difference in the children's conceptions can be seen as illustrating a more active (via their own activity) or a more passive (via an intermediary) view of learning (Pramling, 1986b).

A follow-up study was made of the groups six months after the shop theme was completed. It was then shown that the differences between the experimental groups and the other two groups were even greater. Table 1 illustrates the distribution of the conceptions among the different groups with regard to what they think they have learnt in preschool before the theme was taken up and six months later.

Table 1. <u>Children's conceptions of what they have learnt in preschool before theme (1) and after 6 months (2)</u>

	Group					
	A		B		C	
Occasion	1	2	1	2	1	2
Don't know	3	0	1	2	2	4
To do	16	1	17	15	13	9
To know	0	14	1	0	2	3
To understand	1	2	0	0	0	0
Number of children	20	17	19	17	17	16

There were several children in each group who were not interviewed on the second occasion. Only one child in the experimental group (A) was unable to recall anything, that is, <u>what</u> he had learnt that was more advanced than learning to do something. In one of the other groups (C) there were three children who perceived that they had learnt to know something, and in group B no child was able to think of anything apart from learning to do something. There is also an obvious difference with regard to <u>how</u> one goes about learning something. Now a quarter of the children in the experimental group express that they perceive that they can learn something by thinking, which is a very advanced conception in this age-group (Pramling, 1983a). That the children in the experimental group developed their conceptions still further may probably be explained by the fact that their teacher went on thematising the learning aspect throughout the year (without knowing that a follow-up study would be made) because she thought it was meaningful.

2.2.4 The relationship cognition - metacognition

The purpose of the main study described in this publication is to discover whether children who are in some sense "more aware" (have a qualitatively more advanced conception) of their learning also learn to learn in another way. In order to study this, a special way of working was introduced in two child groups (A and B). This way of working means, firstly, that what the children have experienced of something is always the point of departure for their learning, that is, one assumes that children have thoughts and ideas about what they want to learn. Secondly, it means that the teacher has a didactic goal in the form of what phenomena she wants the children to develop an understanding of. Thirdly, it means that children reflect both at different levels of generality and at a metacognitive level. To help children to develop an understanding of the world around them by varying the levels to which their attention is drawn may be seen as a vertical teaching method, in contrast to a horizontal one in which you keep to a general level and present facts or provide an opportunity for reflection at a general or a specific level.

There is perhaps no need to expand on what reflecting on the specific content and on one's own learning means (see page 16). Structures, on the other hand, need explaining. Structures do not exist in children's thinking in themselves, nor do they exist in the content to be learned. Structures are created by the child when it thinks about something (Marton, 1988). Children create their own structures on the basis of development and experience. This implies that they relate different things to each other, that is, perceive various relationships. One example is what children think happens to the money they hand over when they go shopping. Some children see the handing over of money as a ritual. You hand over money but you get just as much in return. Other children understand that, as a customer, you must hand over money in the shop, that is, they perceive the flow of money to the shop. Yet other children understand that not only is there a flow of money to the shop but also from the shop to the supplier. These two flows of money, however, live an independent life unrelated to each other Ultimately, children understand that it is the customer's money that the shop then uses to buy merchandise (Jahoda, 1979; Pramling, 1986b). What the children have done is simply to create different structures, that is, perceived different relationships. Understanding is, of course, just a question of relating something to something else.

The two teachers involved in the experiment have used the didactic method of working employed in the earlier study concerned with developing children's conceptions of learning (Pramling, 1986b). Two other child groups have functioned as control groups (C and D). Thus, Teachers A and

B have adopted a different way of working than the other teachers throughout a complete school year.

The most general structure forming the basis for understanding is the ability to relate one thing to another. This can mean developing an understanding for relations between the whole and its parts, to understand relations in a cycle, to understand how things are connected in the form of functions, or that there is a connection between cause and effect, that is, one state explains another. This means that the teacher must ponder over what more general structures will arise out of working with concrete things and what activities must be included to make these structures apparent. The didactic implications of this study spring from an idea that the way children think about a content must be the starting-point for educational activitiy. In this way, understanding can also be described in precise terms.

To sum up, the aim of this year's study is to try to develop children's thinking at three different levels of generality. On the one hand, the objective is to try to develop the way children think about their own learning. This can be seen as the most general level of learning. On the other hand, there is also a structural level here, which means that fundamental structures can be found in different contents. This is a level with less generality than conceptions of learning but with greater generality than the third level, which is the content. The didactic approach consists in alternating between these levels. When you work with conceptions of learning or with structures, this is always done in relation to a content. Consequently, the point of this way of working is the simultaneousness of the levels and the alternation between them.

The aim of this study is thus to find out whether children who have been involved in this form of educational activity are better prepared for learning (understanding a new content) than children who have taken part in a more traditional type of preschool programme.

PART 2. METHODS AND IMPLEMENTATION

3. METHODOLOGICAL APPROACH

Instead of a series of more limited experiments, the study is based on the whole situation, of which various aspects can be distinguished later. The study is designed as an experiment in reality, in which the independent variable is a specific didactic approach based on a vertical variation in children's reflections in different teaching situations. Since the experiment is conducted in the everyday setting, it is necessary to violate the rules of traditional experimental design implying that variables should be kept under control. In that kind of experiment one works with various competences to discover a causal relationship, that is, to determine the decisive factor underlying some effect. This is, of course, impossible in everyday situations. The aim is rather to describe different didactic approaches to see what may be achieved in an educational sense. Even if this descriptive approach cannot, strictly speaking, predict what effects are obtained in the form of children's understanding, it can provide the teacher with a practical guideline. Marton (1986) is of the opinion that, since the students' conceptions of learning have a bearing on how they describe and get involved in a learning situation, it is necessary for anyone doing research to decide what type of learning conception best serves the type of learning one desires to develop in the student. Similarly, one should determine how various ways of working affect what children learn, even if it is impossible to establish children's understanding as a direct effect of the teacher's actions with absolute certainty. In other words, it is a question of obtaining detailed information, not of testing relationships.

Methodologically, the project is based on the phenomenographic tradition (Marton, 1981). Phenomenography is concerned with describing people's conceptions of various phenomena in the world around them. The conceptions have been described in the form of qualitatively different categories, characterised by different ways of thinking about various phenomena in the world around us. Phenomenography differs from other educational research in the way research problems are defined.

Phenomenography may be primarily regarded as a methodological approach, that is, a way of collecting and analysing data in order to describe the variation in the ways of thinking expressed by people in relation to a specific content and context. This research approach is descriptive in character and the main results consist of categories of description. People's understanding of something is related to internal explanations, meaning that this understanding is a question of how individuals distinguish and understand something (Säljö, 1982; Pramling, 1983b). The internalist model of explanation may be contrasted with the externalist one, in which external conditions, such as social class or sex, account for the differences in people's ways of thinking (Bernstein, 1971; Dahlberg, 1985).

Phenomenography focuses on revealing people's conceptions as expressed in their statements. These conceptions of various phenomena are, in many respects, already formed during the preschool period on the basis of the experience the children then gain. Learning presupposes certain foundations. The more elementary and self-evident these foundations are, the greater risk that they will be taken for granted in adulthood. It is probably obvious to most teachers that you can learn by acquiring some knowledge about something, but this is not at all apparent to preschool children. Only about 10 per cent of the seven-year-olds and about a quarter of the children who have attended school for a whole year spontaneously connect learning with knowing about or gaining knowledge of something.

The description of children's conceptions is based on data collected by means of the type of clinical interview Piaget developed in his research (Piaget, 1975), that is, interviews that should be clearly aiming at the sort of information the researcher requires, as well as being flexible and capable of following children's ideas as far as possible (Doverborg & Pramling, 1985). All the data are taped and transcribed verbatim.

The analysis then consists of reading all the interviews repeatedly in order to discover similarities and differences between the conceptions. When a pattern in the form of qualitatively different ways of thinking about a certain phenomena begins to crystallise, then it is time to systematically re-read all the interviews to check that they are all covered by the pattern. If this does not turn out to be the case, one must continue to work on the data until all the conceptions are described in the categories one has discovered. The main thing is to try to see things in the child's perspective all the time. It is a question of a contextual analysis in the sense that the focus is on children's thinking about a particular content. There must be a close connection between empirical data and the ways of describing children's conceptions. Furthermore, the categories of description should naturally not overlap each another (Larsson, 1986).

In order to analyse and attempt to understand what something looks like to a child, it is necessary to know about child development in general as well as being acquainted with the preschool and the activity the child has been involved in. In other words, the researcher needs to have a clear idea of the child's frame of reference.

What children express in an interview situation can depend on how they perceive what they are involved in. That is why the teachers in the different preschools carried out a final interview in the last few days of the spring term with the purpose of finding out how they had perceived my presence in their school. Hundeide (1987) has shown how he believes children interpret different experimental situations on the basis of how they "understand the scene", that is, the situation, expectations (their own and that of others), what "contracts" they have entered into with the interviewer and how they see themselves and their role in the situation. According to Hundeide, children quite simply play different roles depending on how they have understood the scene. In Hundeide's case, he has allowed the normal teacher to enter the experimental situation while the leader of the experiment is called to the telephone. The teacher then asks the children to show and give an account of what they are doing and enquires about the questions the leader of the experiment has put to them.

My situation, that of a researcher who has observed the children in various ways throughout the year, is of course not comparable with Hendeide's, whose experiments were of a limited nature. Nor were the children questioned immediately after the situation they were involved in but after a whole year of observations and numerous interviews. The questions the children were confronted with were: "Why do you think Ingrid was here in preschool so often? Why has she interviewed you so often?" To describe the children's ideas about these points here may appear to anticipate the presentation of the results, but I have chosen to do so because it is a methodological issue.

There are qualitative differences in the children's answers to the question: "Why has Ingrid been here?" Some children think that the reason for the researcher's visit is that she is to <u>learn</u> what they are doing in preschool, sing songs etc. This is an idea that may perhaps be attributed to the fact that all the preschools have student teachers from time to time who are there specifically to learn. Other ideas are that I am doing research or that I am interested in <u>how children think</u>, that I have been there to interview them, or to find out <u>what they know</u>. The children who say that I want to know how much they know refer to the school world in some cases. Yet other children appear to have understood that I have been there to <u>teach them</u> something, or to <u>help</u> them. Some children do not know.

As we see in Table 2, some children have given more than one reason, which explains why the number of reasons exceeds the number of children.

Table 2. <u>The reason for the researcher's visit</u>

	Preschool			
	A	B	C	D
Learn	10	5	6	10
Children's ideas	1	4	-	-
Interviewed	6	5	1	4
What we know	1	3	2	1
Teach or help us	4	4	3	2
Don't know	1	1	6	2
Number of children	19	21	18	17

About half the children in both the A and D groups have thought that I had been there to learn. This is also the most common idea in groups B and C, even if only a quarter of the children in group B and a third of those in group C expressed it.

The children's ideas about why I visited the preschool recur in the answers to the question why they were interviewed, in that they say that I <u>want to know</u> something (how children think, what they are doing and what they think about something, or what the children have learnt). Another idea is that I think it is <u>fun</u> (this includes the idea that the interview is to serve as a record of them, or that someone is going to listen to it).

Table 3. <u>Why they were interviewed</u>

| | Preschool | | | |
	A	B	C	D
Want to know	12	11	11	11
Fun	2	2	2	2
Don't know	5	2	5	4
Number of children	19	15(6)	18	17

In Table 3 we see that 6 children in the B group have not been given this question. More than half the children in all the groups think that the purpose of the interviews is that I want to know something. Just as many in the A, C and D groups do not know why they have been interviewed. Between 5 and 7 children in all the groups believe that they have been interviewed because I wanted to know what they know or have learnt in preschool.

As we have seen in Tables 2 and 3, ideas varied as to why the researcher had visited the preschool and why they had been interviewed. However, no marked difference can be observed between the experimental and control groups, so that these ideas cannot be related to the results of the study either. In practice, the children in all the groups have generally treated me as one of their teachers, in that they often came up to me and asked about things just as they did with their normal teacher.

3.1 Study subjects

<u>The teachers</u>
Four part-time preschools and all their children participated in the study. Besides the preschool teacher, there was a nursery nurse attached to each of the preschools, but since the preschool teacher not only has the formal educational responsibility but was also shown to have it in reality in the groups, I am referring to the preschool teacher when using the term teacher.

The teachers were chosen because they were "known" to be competent, either through their seniors in the administration or through the teacher training programme, since they are all supervisors for new students. All the teachers agreed to participate without much hesitation. It should be mentioned, however, that one of the teachers was asked several weeks after term had started because another teacher had backed out. None of the teachers had worked for less than 10 years in a group of children, while one had almost 20 years' experience. Teacher A had already taken part, in her capacity as preschool teacher, in another study in the project in which an attempt was made to develop conceptions of learning (see page 18).

The teachers were interviewed about what things they thought were important for children to learn in preschool and about how they carried out their work. They were required not only to talk about their work but to reflect on children's learning. At the end of the school year they all wrote down some reflections on what it had been like to participate in the project.

The preschool groups

Preschools A, B and C are situated in mixed residential areas with terraced and detached houses in different parts of Göteborg and its suburbs. Preschools A and C occupy detached houses. Preschool D occupies the ground floor of a 3-storey block of flats and its catchment area includes areas of detached houses and rented flats. Preschool B is situated next to a lower and middle compulsory school. The preschool that was selected as comparable with preschool B backed out of the project after several weeks following information to parents and the interview with the teacher. The reason for withdrawal was that the teacher said she wanted in work "in peace" with the children.

Table 4. <u>The number of children at the four preschools at the first interview</u>

Preschool	A	B	C	D
Number of children	19	20	18	19
Boys/girls	9/10	11/9	8/10	12/7
2nd year in preschool	3	9	12	5
5-year-olds	-	-	6	6
6-year-olds	19	19	11	13
7-year-olds	-	1	1	-
Average age	6:3	6:5	5:10	5:10
Variation	5:10-6:8	5:11-6:10	4:11-6:9	4:10-6:6

As we see in Table 4, the groups are similar in size. The number stated in the table refers to the children who were there at the first interview in the autumn term. During the autumn a child who was moved back from school joined group B. Two children joined group C after the Christmas holidays. On the whole, boys and girls were evenly distributed, with the exception of group D, where boys predominated. In preschool A only a few children had already attended the previous year, compared with about a quarter in group D, barely half in group B and two-thirds in group C. In groups C and D there were six five-year-olds, which means that the average age and the variation in age here differ from those in groups A and B.

The control group that backed out was made up entirely of six-year-olds. However, anyone doing research in the everyday situation must accept the fact that it is not always possible to control things in real life. While working on the project, I often wondered whether I should exclude the five-year-olds in my presentation of the results. But for one thing the number of children would then have varied, making any comparison difficult, for another, the context for the six-year-olds in groups C and D is, of course, different because they have younger children in the group, whether their conceptions are described or not. Analysis of the data has, however, shown that it was impossible to detect any systematic difference between the five- and six-year-olds, so that I have included both in my account. In the appendix, however, the more important tables show the five- and six-year-olds from the groups C and D groups separately. (The numbers of the tables in the appendix correspond to those in the results section).

3.2 Collection of data

The amount of data collected is considerable. It consists partly of <u>observations</u> in various types of learning situations and recorded in narrative form. These observations were made one day per week in preschools A and B, one day per fortnight (sometimes more often) in C and D. In addition, all the teachers have themselves taped various forms of conversation to a certain extent. However, only a few recordings are available from group C because of technical hitches. The recordings have been made to obtain both a wider selection showing what happens in the learning situations and a more detailed picture of the content. The observations have always comprised the class sessions and the activities that are usually organised by the teachers in connection with them. Besides these, spontaneous play situations have been observed and recorded, as well as information about how the teachers have planned activities throughout the year.

The other large body of data consists of <u>interviews</u> and various forms of <u>learning experiments</u> with the children. The children were interviewed separately a total of eight times in the course of the preschool year, and their first interview took place within a few weeks of starting preschool.(Information had been sent out to the parents, but only one of them telephoned and wanted to have additional information). The final interview was conducted by the teachers. Thus, the basic data material now comprises about 580 interviews. It was not possible to interview all the children on all occasions, because someone was always sick or away on holiday. Some omissions are due to the child being absent during the activity on which the interview was based. Having four groups meant that it was simply impossible to find the time to return and follow up individual children. <u>Drawings</u> were collected in connection with some of the interviews. Finally, the children were given a <u>reading test.</u> (These tests will be commented on in a forthcoming publication). The reason why I collected in the reading tests was that I had noticed that the work on language skills varied greatly from teacher to teacher.

I had visited the groups even before I started interviewing so that the children would recognise me. One interview was carried out at the beginiing of the autumn ternn and all the rest were conducted during the spring term. All the the interviews were held individually in a room at the preschool.

As far as following up the learning experiments is concerned, an assistant who did not know which were the experimental groups and which were the control groups was responsible. The reason for this was that I did not want my expectations to affect the results. The various interviews differ both as to content and purpose, so that they will be described in detail in each section of the results. Two of the interviews deal mainly with children's learning. Three interviews are conducted after the children have taken part in learning experiments. One interview is aimed at obtaining the child's view of the researcher's visit (see page 26) and, finally, two deal with "The shop theme" (which is not presented here).

3.3. Cooperation in the preschools studied

Teachers A and B have worked with me in so far as we set up goals together for what we wanted to try to achieve with the children during the year in the form of mental insight. One of the goals has been to encourage children to reflect on their own learning by thinking about what they are doing, and about how and why they are doing it. The other has been to try to develop children's understanding by getting them to understand certain structures and reflect on their content.

After discussions with each teacher we agreed that teacher A should work primarily with trying to get children to recognise structures in the form of a cycle, visible to the children, while teacher B should concentrate on clarifying structures in the form of cause and effect. This has meant that constant discussions have taken place between the project leader and the teachers about how this could be clearly demonstrated in the normal preschool programme.The point of departure was always the teacher's own planning.

Both these teachers have had a response to their work in that we have discussed children's reactions and behaviour in relation to what they have done. They have also been allowed to listen to interviews and to study my observations. Both have been very interested and have even familiarised themselves with my earlier research.

If as a researcher I should reflect on how cooperation has succeeded, I can say that teacher A seemed to have an advantage in that she had previously made some attempt to work in accordance with the ideas on which this didactic approach is based. She quite simply found it easier to adapt her working methods and content to the principles we tried to develop in the project.Teacher B proved to be very good at creating situations and putting questions to children in order to get them to reflect, but has not been able to follow her didactic intentions as resolutely. Furthermore, teacher B's work situation was rather complex. She was not only helping to draw up guidelines for preschool activities in the local authority area (autumn term) but attending continuation courses in the evening. She also had an ambitious programme for working with languages and cooperated with school to a wide extent. All these activities meant that her energy was somewhat divided.

3.4 Implementation

This account of the how the research project was implemented is based on my own observations and on the interviews with the teachers. The subject areas dealt with in the different groups during the year are also described. By subject areas is meant the content (theme) planned by the teacher and which the children have worked with for varying lengths of time. During class sessions, which are to be found in all the preschools, numerous other subjects for discussion have, of course, arisen spontaneously . As far as the way of working is concerned, I have tried to bring out the characteristics of each preschool using my observations and tape-recordings as a basis.

3.4.1 Interviews of teachers at the beginning of term

Teacher A points out that children already know a lot, such as, for example, counting to 10, colours, etc, when they begin preschool. So it is more a question of observing during play whether they know what the figure five or the amount three looks like. One will have to practise more with those who do not know this by, for example, playing games with them. It is important for the teacher to know a great deal about children's development in different areas, so that this provides a frame of reference for the work.

Children should be introduced to the "school world" with care so that this does not turn out to be a shock to them. Typical of the school world is that you have to function in a group, sit still, follow instructions, choose, take initiative, etc, so that these aspects must be included in the activities. As far as the content, in the forms of themes that vary from year to year, is concerned, it is important to see the whole and to work at helping the children to understand. You have to begin with the children's own experience and knowledge and work towards developing their insight. The teacher realises that she has become more and more aware over the years that you should never take it for granted that children have understood or grasped something you have been talking about. This has led her to work in small groups because, as she says, you then have a greater chance of reaching more children.

Teacher B also points out how important it is to find out the children's level of development at the beginning of term. She divides the work between the social aspects and knowledge aspects. The social part covers waiting one's turn, playing together, solving conflicts, showing consideration and taking responsibility. The part concerned with knowledge deals largely with making good use of children's knowledge so as to get them to mature and feel that they are able to do things. The important thing is to inspire children to learn by having an exploratory type of working method and interesting material and to answer children's questions. Part of the preparation for school includes working with numbers and the alphabet and explaining why it it is important to learn to read. If you provide the material, many children learn to read, she thinks. With regard to the themes, the teacher expressed some dissatisfaction with some of the previous themes, which were poorly planned and too much "above the children's heads". She points out that it is important that children are allowed to observe and study things and that the teacher talks less. The change she notices in her own work is particularly her awareness of children's lack of understanding when the teacher gives the traditional type of instruction (talks too much). She says she asks children much more and tries to find out what they think about certain things and they are are allowed to think out things to a much greater extent than before.

Teacher C takes up social aspects and says that it is important for children to learn to be away from their mothers, learn to follow instructions, listen, observe, concentrate, be independent and able to dress themselves, be alone out in the playground and know what one may or may not do. She also considers all these social aspects as preparation for school, as well as learning to handle paper, pencil and scissors. The themes they take up relate to nature, the immediate environmnet or colour and form. These recur year after year, although some attempt is made to vary them. But as the teacher says, children understand them in different ways, since they are at different stages of maturity. As far as any change in her own situation is concerned, the teacher thinks that people are beginning to revert to the working methods that prevailed when she was training many years ago.

Teacher D also emphasises social aspects, such as, for example, that it is important that they feel secure in the group, that they are able to be with children of the same age, to wait for their turn, follow instructions and feel responsibility. They should quite simply feel that what they are doing is serious, that they have to achieve something and finish things properly. Children learn a great deal through play, but it is important to know what stage of development the children have reached so as to adapt the tasks to their capacity. The teacher goes on to say that they have different themes every year, but the aim is, of course, to produce the same insight (about the seasons, animals and ourselves). It is important to have a long-term work programme and to return to the same things. The change she sees in her own attitude is that she stresses learning more than formerly and that she has discovered that children possess a great deal of knowledge. She has also been inspired by Montessori, particularly with regard to the written word and self-instructive material.

All the teachers emphasise the social aspect of preschool. All of them also say that they work with themes. Teachers A and D vary these from year to year, but they are nevertheless aimed at developing the same insight. Teacher B also varies her themes, but expresses some dissatisfaction with those of previous years. Teacher C says she has the same themes because children change. Teachers A and B claim to have become more observant of how children perceive the world around them and they have realised how difficult it is to get children to understand, while believing that children already know a great deal when they start preschool. Teacher D now stresses the learning aspect more than previously, and also that children are very knowledgeable. Teacher C now places more emphasis on children's maturity and believes that the traditional preschool education methods are about to be reinstated.

3.4.2 The teachers' comments after data were collected

<u>Teacher A</u> thinks that the year has been informative and exciting. She also thinks that she has learnt not to underestimate children's knowledge and to listen to them more, even though she thought she had done this before, too, but perhaps the teaching method had more the character of instruction than now. She feels she has been given a "kick forward", in that the has become more observant of what is happening in the group. The teacher also points out that it was sometimes laborious and difficult finding out what I wanted to bring out. Finally, she says that the children have felt fine and the group has functioned well as a result of the way they have worked..

<u>Teacher B</u> says that the combination of reading and reflecting on children's learning on the basis of what I have written and working practically at the same time has been instructive. "I have quite simply understood children's learning in different connections better", she says. To think out and plan themes more carefully makes it easier to carry them out. The special theme "The Shop" produced new impulses and much response on the part of the children. Taking part in children's games provided insight into their way of thinking and solving problems. Their view of reality became apparent and many opportunities arose in which to impart some knowledge to the children. The children appreciated having the teachers with them. The conversations with the children were interesting, but unfortunately many spontaneous conversations were not recorded. In the end some children thought it was a bit boring with tape-recordings. It has been an instructive year, which was both hard work and fun, was teacher B's comment. The most difficult thing was, not to lose sight of the main purpose in all the different activities.

<u>Teacher C</u> says that she feels only positive about having taken part in the project. She feels privileged to be able to have contact with education and research. The teacher also points out that the children thought that it was exciting to take part in the interviews. The only thing that she really felt was a little difficult was the shop theme, because it was something that they had neither planned themselves nor introduced on the initiative of the children. But she also says that some of the children in the group continued to play shop long after the theme was ended and that the "old" children from last year are now asking about the shop.

<u>Teacher D</u> says that the visits have not been at all obtrusive. But when I came without warning and they had not planned things properly (which did not, in fact, often happen), they had a bit of a conscience. The teacher says this was because they were a little uncertain about the purpose of my visit (although they had been informed that I was observing them in order to compare different ways of working and to find out about the way the children thought about various things developed). "But we also feel curious", she says. "When the visits were planned it felt better. In some way it was then easier to keep to the point and follow the plan".........

In conclusion, it can be said that teachers A and B feel that they themselves have gained some benefit from collaborating with me. They say it has been difficult at times. To question one's work and to look for new ways <u>is</u> difficult! Teacher D expresses some uncertainty about my presence, because she has not known exactly what my purpose was. Teacher C does not express any uncertainty but certainly a little distaste for including something they have not planned themselves. All the teachers have been very obliging and helpful.

3.4.3 The content worked with in the different preschools

<u>Preschool A</u>
The autumn term began with several weeks' work about the children themselves and their homes. This was followed by a theme about rain and water, which lasted well into the spring term. The three stages the theme focussed on were: 1) nature (clouds, weather signs, rain, snow, hail, rainbow, the need of plants for water, etc.), 2) man (use of water, where it goes to, how it enters our houses, purifying plants), 3) the relationship between nature and man (our dependence on water, pollution). This was followed by several shorter sessions about spring, which took the form of sowing seeds, planting potatoes, etc. The shop theme took over after that. One student teacher introduced the theme on fish (the sea, fishing tackle, fish shop, food). The spring term ended with the bee as a theme (from the bee to fruit, the bee colony, seasons etc.).

<u>Preshool B</u>
The first weeks began with the children getting to know each other (names, etc.) and the rules that applied in the preschool (i.e. what one is allowed, not allowed to do). They worked with colours for a while, did a lot of painting

and learnt about different techniques. After this the sun was a general theme, returning again and again during most of the year. In the autumn term this involved taking up the changes in nature in the autumn (berries, vegetables, flowers, etc.) which were related to the sun and sunlight. Other subjects dealt with during the autumn were cultural, theatre, books (library). Clothes were also discussed. In the spring term the theme on the sun was resumed, now in relation to winter. They took up different sources of heat (old and new). Time was related to the sun, as was food. Animals (small birds and insects), traffic, the shop, hospital were other subjects. The year ended with spring, which meant that it was possible to link up with the sun once again.

Preschool C

Besides naturally working with learning the children's names, etc., the first area studied was colour and form. The next theme was "Our natural surroundings". The preschool has woods close by and the tree was therefore selected for more detailed study, automatically leading to the season, autumn. During the autumn they also found time for the child, the family and certain work places (hairdresser, optician, baker, interior decorator), all of which, however, continued into the spring term. Winter and spring were other seasons that were taken up. The shop was a subject, and also the book and how it is made.

Preschool D

In this preschool, too, they began by taking up the children's names etc., and colour and form. But the general theme throughout the year concerned animals and nature during the different seasons. During the autumn they worked with fruit (e.g. the apple) and vegetables (root vegetables, cabbage, etc.). The life and habits of animals studied were; elk (elk hunting), birds (starling, cuckoo, willy wagtail, lapwing, pied flycatcher) and animals that hibernate (bear, hedgehog, mice). During the autumn they also found time for traffic, the thermometer, the numbers 1 - 10, rain and rainbow, a good and a bad playmate, narcotics and war toys. In the spring term they began with a theme about the shop, then returned to animals and nature, which now dealt with animals tracks, cones and coniferous trees, more birds (blue tit, bullfinch, hedge sparrow) and roedeer. As a change from animals and nature, they took up the time, clock and measurements of length. Besides looking at spring flowers (coltsfoot, liverwort, and wood anemones), several different food chain were dealt with (in the coniferous forest, leaf-earthworm-hen, etc.). The animals studied were the hen family, the spider, the ant and the anthill, the ladybird, the butterfly, earthworms and the bee.

One can conclude by saying that what strikes one most is the great difference between the preschools as regards both what they cover during a school year and the number of different things. Despite this, one can say that there is a core content that all (3 of the 4) take up. I would say that this is the seasons and the subjects associated with it, climate and animals. Another one is the child, the family and the home or the immediate environment. Colour and form also appears to have an accepted place in the preschool. One can wonder why, of course. As we know, this was included in the earliest infant schools (Infant Schools, 1837). Colour and form has also long constituted an important element in many kinds of psychological tests. Nearly all children know the primary colours when they start preschool. One of the teachers tested this at the beginning, but they worked with them all the same. As far as the forms were concerned, it was shown in an earlier study that very few children learnt to name them correctly, even though they concentrated on them for a whole week (Pramling, 1986a). For children there is simply no point in learning these names, and trying to commit square, circle, triangle and rectangle to memory is a meaningless exercise. Colours or forms are a part of many games in the preschool, but all that is required to play these is generally the ability to recognise similarities (between colours or forms), not to know their names.

In addition, all groups have made trips to such cultural activities as, the theatre, concerts or museums or visited a farm, and these have naturally been brought up and discussed at the time. Other things they have in common, and which have not been mentioned, are traditions in connection with various festivals (Lucia, Christmas, Easter, etc.). Another tradition, which is perhaps the most widespread one of all in the preschools, is that of making drawings for anyone celebrating their birthday. Another subject they have in common concerns school, letters of the alphabet and numbers. In particular, they all share such as activities as sewing, weaving, baking, drawing, modelling in plasticine, carpentry and building. These have always been a part of the preschool programme (Doverborg & Johansson, 1986).

3.4.4 Ways of working in the different preschools

<u>Preschool A</u>
The A group is characterised by an exploratory method of working, in which the teacher creates many opportunities and situations for the children as a basis for their own reflections. The class sessions with the whole group vary as to content. Sometimes it is a matter of discussing something connected with the theme they are working with. At other times they play educational games of various kinds, for example, with letters and numbers. Or it can be a question of telling someone who has been away all about what they have been doing, or a child may take up some item of news, such as, for example, that grandfather has been admitted to hospital. This is developed into a talk about death, etc., for a period of 20 minutes.

Both class sessions and various activities generally have a definite purpose in the form of what the teacher wants to get the children to reflect on, which is partly their own learning and partly the structure in the form of relationships between various things, relationships which should sometimes be seen as a cycle. Sometimes this is achievedin the form of discussions, but generally concrete tasks are given. The children seldom sit at the tables all together. Some activities are prolonged, as, for example, when they are making a millipede out of pieces of cardboard. Children who are interested in sewing often have projects, such as sewing balls, pencil cases, etc. Many of the activities are documented in the children's books, which they sometimes call their encyclopaedias. The children are confronted with many questions, bringing out the features of their world.

One example of creating situations on which to reflect is when they work with the theme "Rain and water". Four children at a time may sit in a room with the teacher. They are each given a piece of paper which they are requested to fold in half. They are given the task of making a drawing on one side showing <u>good</u> weather, and one on the other side showing <u>bad</u> weather. When they are ready, they are allowed to compare their drawings and then discover with the help of teacher's questions the relativity of what is fine and bad weather. To mother bad weather may be when she has to pull little brother in his pram through the snow (someone has drawn this). The children, on the other hand, think of this weather as fine, because they can, for example, build igloos and go tobogganing. Other aspects are the flower that is happy when it rains, while an adult might get annoyed when he is splashed by a passing car. The teacher's message that there is neither good nor bad weather except in relation to someone or something then becomes apparent to the children. Here the children not only reflect on the phenomenon good or bad weather, but also on how different children think in different ways, as expressed in their drawings.

Another example is when the teacher wants to make the children aware that symbols are something people have invented to facilitate communication. The children are given a task to draw some symbols for "high pressure", "low pressure" (which they have talked about), cold air, warm air, thunder, storm and sunshine. The children are urged to think of some good symbols themselves. When everybody has done this, the teacher then hangs up all the children's drawings in a row so as to compare them with the symbols used by a popular weather forecaster, which she has in a book, as well as looking at the similarities and differences among the children's own drawings. This leads to much discussion on how to draw symbols - nearly all the children have drawn the same ones in some cases and quite different in others - and why it is that some of the children's symbols are much clearer (easier to understand) than those on the official weather map.

As we have seen in these two examples about weather and symbols, the children first have to use their imagination and form an idea about something. In the next stage the children are made aware of each other's ideas, i.e. the variation in their ways of thinking is brought out. This method of alternating between the cognitive and metacognitive levels is one that permeates most of the year's programme.

On another occasion the children have been given the task of trying to find out what snowflakes look like and then to draw them. They compare them and say that all snowflakes have six points, but despite this they all have different patterns, just as people are all different. "If you think about what we talked about in the auturm, how the rain comes, how do you think then that we get snow in the winter?" Someone says , "The water drops clump together and turn into ice crystals." Someone else says, "Well, it's the same cycle as the rain." Teacher, "And then there's snow instead of rain just because it is colder in the winter." They all look at the wall chart that they had made on a previous occasion of the cycle of rain and water. Now their attention is focussed on the structure in the form of relationships (the cycle).

"How is it that we get rain and snow really?" They have to solve this problem is small groups. The different solutions are discussed and compared. "Shall we see how many different ways of thinking why we get snow and rain there are in your solutions?" The attention is now at the metacognitive level, i.e. how they think about structures.

The next step comes on another occasion when the teacher asks, "Have you ever wondered how we get drinking water into our houses?" Someone says, "Through the pipes." "It comes to the purifying plant first," says another. Teacher then asks, "Where does it come from to the purifying plant?" "From the sea, I think." "The pipes go down in the ground." Teacher, "Why are they buried?" "So we don't trip over them and so they don't get broken." Teacher asks whether they remember that they got a hole in a water pipe last year so that nobody in the neighbourhood had any water. They talk about this for a while. Teacher asks what they use water for and the children make suggestions: washing, doing the dishes, drinking, flushing the toilet, mixing cordial, etc. They observe that they have thought of many different things. Teacher, "Where does the water go to then?" "Out into the sea," says one. "Do they purify it?" asks teacher. "Yes, you have to because it is poisonous." Teacher, "What would happen otherwise?" The discussion takes up the problems of the fish dying and the factories not always purifying their water. While the children are talking about how this purification is done, teacher draws on a large sheet of paper on the wall so that the cycle can be seen clearly. First attention has been paid to how children think about water, then again to the structure as a cycle.

Many days are then spent in creating a picture of a town with all its "underworld" (water pipes and drains). At regular intervals the teacher gets then to ponder over how the water goes round in the same way as they talked about on the subject of rain and water. They have also made various experiments with steam to illustrate and create situations to reflect on. When doing the experiments, the children had to think about why they were doing them and whether they could do them in another way to find out about rain and water (the learning aspect).

Yet another task was to "invent" something, i.e. a toy that doesn't exist. Four children at a time sit at a table with the teacher. The children have paper and crayons and are urged to draw what they think of. "What do you do to invent something?" asks the teacher. Someone says, "You can think of something that you would like yourself and make it up." Some of the groups ponder and reflect a great deal, while others sit silently and doggedly with their task. Afterwards the teacher puts up all the children's drawings, and they talk together about what the children have invented, how they thought when they invented their "thing", whether they usually think out anything else and, if so, what.

In this example, we see not only that the children have to imagine something and observe the variation, but also the third level, that is, that their attention is turned towards themselves and their ability to think (learn).

To get children to reflect on their own learning and on how they think about it, they were asked one day to ponder over what the weather would be like the following day. After these reflections they were then given the task of finding out for the following day several ways of forecasting the weather. The next day, after they have given an account of various observations and signs that can be found in nature for predicting the weather, the teacher asks them what they did to find out about these things. One has asked his mother, another his grandfather, Per has read a book, Ulla has seen a programme on TV and Elin says she has "worked it out" by herself. The teacher then points out to the children how many different ways of finding out what the weather would be like they were able to think out. "Are there any other ways of finding out what you want to know?" The reflections are now at a metacognitive level, that is, how they think about what can be learnt.

In conclusion, the structure of the work can be illustrated by two examples in which the main points are set out:

The theme "Rain and water"

1. Children's reflections on and conceptions of rain and water (content) in combination with experiments. The teacher's help with noticing the variation in the ways of thinking (in words or with pictures).

2. Children's attention is directed towards the structure in the form of the cycle, and their reflections on this.

3. Children's attention is directed towards what they are experimenting with, talking about and drawing, how and why they are doing it, and whether there are any other ways of learning (thinking out, finding out, doing, obtaining information, etc.) , that is, towards their own learning.

At all three levels, they change their perspective from time to time with the teacher's help by reflecting on how they think about the content, structure and learning. The same stages recur in relation to water supply and sewers in a town.

The theme "The bee and the bee colony"

1. Children's reflections on the life and habits of the bee, what it eats, where it lives, etc. Attention is drawn to the variation, for example, that children have several different ideas about where the bee lives, how it lives, etc. (the content).

2. Children's attention is directed towards the relationship between bees and plants. "If there weren't any plants, what would bees eat?" "If there weren't any bees, would we get any fruit?" (These are two questions that the teacher had in mind for bringing out the mutual dependence as a relationship.) Continues with the yearly changes in the bee, forming a kind of cycle (the structure), to which the children's attention is drawn.

3. Children's attention is directed towards how you find out more about bees, what they can do themselves in order to find out, etc. (learning).

Preschool B

The work in group B is concentrated and lively, that is, there are always many different activities in progress. A class session is held daily when the children arrive. It usually concerns letters of the alphabet, words, sentences, numbers. Sometimes a child comes up with a topic and the teacher expands on it. For example, a child might say that he going to Mexico. The teacher then takes this up and asks the children how do they think he is going to get there. A long discussion ensues on distances, bridges and means of transport. Other types of discussion take place later in the day, either when all the children are gathered, or in half the group or a third of the group (about 7 children). Meanwhile the other children are usually engaged in some activity such as painting or modelling with plasticine. Much time is spent on different techniques. The work in the group has been characterised by constant discussions in which the teacher tries to get the children to think out and reflect on a variety of things.

Another rather common feature was that children made up stories and acted little plays for each other. A large group of boys also built with bricks on the floor every day.

An example of children's reflections and discussions is the time when five of them were given the task of drawing the area where they live as seen from a helicopter.The children were creative,they discussed,reasoned, encouraged, criticised and joked with each other. They produced not only a drawing but a whole story about what happened in the area. Later they discussed with the teacher what they had drawn and why just that.

Sometimes the children are given various problems to be solved in the group. One exampls is when various small groups are allowed to discuss and arrive at how to make a letter-box of cardboard. The letter-boxes will then look different, leading to many and lengthy discussions on what letter-boxes look like, why, etc. It becomes apparent that the children have made their letter-boxes according to varying points of view, that is, that of the postal service (everyone has to have the same kind) or that of the individual owner (who wants his letter-box to be as decorative as possible).

What the children have to do here is to reflect, on letter-boxes. The teacher focuses on the variation in the way of thinking about letter-boxes by drawing their attention to the fact they have made three different kinds of letter-box. In the next stage the teacher brings out the structure, in the form of the cause-effect relationship, by asking the children what would happen if all the public letter-boxes did not look alike or why the ones at the entrances to their homes do not have to look alike. In the third stage she introduces the learning aspect by facing the children with the problem of finding out what letter-boxes are like in other countries. They are given the task of asking their parents if they know what letter-boxes look like in any country they have visited (if the children themselves haven't been there). When they come back and report what their parents have said about the appearance of letter-boxes, the teacher goes on to ask them if they would be able to find out what letter-boxes look like in other countries in any other way besides actually going there, etc.

The teacher asks lots of questions. "What is darkness?" Someone replies: "Well, it can't be light all the time!" Teacher: "When is it dark then?" "At night." "Can it be dark at any other time?" "In the winter," says one. Someone talks about how creepy it is when it is dark. "I know why it's dark, you have to rest some time and get more energy," says another. "More energy, what's that?" asks teacher. The conversation turns naturally to people who work at night and what they do in the daytime and teacher asks if you can sleep if it's light. Suddenly a child bursts out, "I know why it's dark, it's just because the earth spins round!" Teacher: "The earth spins round, yes, it does." "Then it's dark somewhere else on earth," someone says. One child tells them that her mother and father have been in Australia and that they telephoned home once when it was night there and day here. They talk about it being dark just then in certain places, morning in some places and evening in others. "I learnt about the sun and earth on the Baloo programme on TV." Teacher continues: "What is darkness? What's missing?" "The sun," one replies. Teacher: "If I get inside a cupboard, isn't the sun shining then?" They go on talking for a long time about lack of light, what it feels like in the dark, etc. "People are a little afraid of the dark, there may be ghosts," says one. Someone talks about people believing in ghosts in the olden days. Another thinks that you are only afraid if you think about nasty things. The discussion is prolonged still further. The teacher's purpose in this discussion is to get the children to reflect on the connection between the sun and light. Then she wants to get the children to understand the relation between the sun and heat. She does this by first getting the children to ponder over the insects and other things they have found in the frozen ground and taken home with them. To make the relationship even more obvious, she asks them what they think will happen to the insects and plants once they are indoors. The children know, of course, that is is warm indoors. But what must happen before it's warm outdoors?

One day they have gone out with speeds and dug up earth and grass under the snow. Back inside they look at what these contain with a magnifying glass. They talk about and study what they have found, insects, flower buds, moss, etc. After this groups of children are given the task of telling the others in some way about the things they have found out. Continuing in three groups and with the teacher's help, one group decides to make a newspaper, another write a letter and the third cardboard dolls with which to act out a story about what they have found. In this case the learning aspect is also apparent in that they are faced with the concrete task of imparting the knowledge they have gained themselves, the way this is achieved naturally varying from group to group.

To illustrate how you can find out things from books, the children make a large number of books themselves. For example. everybody is given the task of drawing something with four legs, something that is round, etc. These drawings are then bound together in a little book, which they keep on their bookshelf. Many children illustrate and write stories with the teacher's help, and these are also bound into books.

Finally, an example from when children talk about food and ponder over what food is. They are allowed to talk about something they like and then draw it on one half of a sheet of paper, while on the other half they are requested to draw the ingredients this food consists of and where they come from. Someone has drawn rice pudding and draws rice that is growing and milk which comes from the cow. Another is fond of pancakes and draws eggs and a hen, milk and a cow and flour coming from plants. All the drawings are presented and discussed and the teacher gradually arrives at her message about the relationship between animals, plants and our food, that is, without animals and plants human beings would not have anything to eat.

We see here that the same idea appears as in previous examples, that is, first the children have to think about where food comes from and listen to each other's ideas (the content). In the next stage the teacher focuses on the structure in the form of a relationship (cause-effect), that is, our food comes from animals and plants. Since many children do not believe that all food comes from animals and plants, they have to go on thinking about it and put forward suggestions about food that does not come from these. How can you find out what does not come from animals or plants (learning)?

Preschool C

In the C group class sessions are not given a central place, but, on the other hand, the children's activities are. After meeting toegther for a short while, the children work at the tables with something out of their lockers. This is usually some large piece of work, such as, for example, sewing a baking cloth or a gym bag or painting baskets or flower pots, besides the more traditional bead mats and weaving. When you have painted your flower pot, you are allowed to sow seeds in it. When you have sown your baking cloth, you can bring the ingredients from home and bake bread. The focus is on making things. The teacher is always available and ready to assist with threading needles, etc., but there are never any models. When the children make finger puppets in the form of insects from gauze soaked in plaster of Paris, they make many kinds of animals. When they make different things out of clay, someone wants to make a pirate. The child and the teacher then look for a book about pirates to be able to study what a pirate looks like. Generally, the teacher has set out all the material for some activity and the class session is spent preparing it, but the major part of the class session is devoted to the children's free associations.

One day a child says, "You are not allowed to whisper in school, are you? My grandfather has told me about being put in a corner." "Being put in a corner, what's that?" asks one. "What was there in the corner?" wonders another. Teacher: "A chair." "But what if three children were naughty at the same time?" The discussion continues for quite a while. Then the teacher shows them a clay pot. "Hurray, we're going to plant something," says one. The teacher then says that they have to paint the pots first, so that they are all different. Someone wonders why, and some moments are spent sorting this out. Then she talks about sowing in earth, about seeds, about watering them and that they have to look after their pots every day. Everybody wants to paint, but teacher selects a few children.

Another example from a class session is when the children start talking about the army and pistols, bacause some child has brought a tiny toy pistol with him. Someone's father is going to be a soldier again, he says, and teacher tells them that this is called a military refresher course. After discussing this for a while, someone says he is going to see his grandmother, who has a little dog. The next topic of conversation is then dogs. When this conversation also comes to an end, teacher says. "You know what it was we have been talking about," holding up her arms. The children cry out "Trunk!" "What's on top?" Someone says, "The tree-top." Teacher continues her questions; "What do you find on the trunk?" "Bark," she answers herself when no one can think of it. She continues: "What is an insect?" The children count out "ant, mosquito, fly and caterpillar." Teacher then says that all insects are caterpillars when they are small, but that different caterpillars turn into different insects. "When the caterpillars sit on the leaves, what are they doing?" "Eating," says one. "Where do they go in winter?" Teacher herself tells them they go back to the bark. "What lives in the tree-top?" The children count out "squirrels and birds." "What can a bird's nest look like?" "What must a tree be like for birds to be able to peck a hole in it?" "What is the thing called that people put up?" "What do the birds collect?" Some child answers the questions all the time. Teacher tells them about somebody who had hung a wool mat outside and that the birds had removed all the wool. All the children listen. Someone talks about a bird that has built a nest in their garden. The teacher goes on with her questions. "What happens to the birds in winter?" She tells them that many of them migrate and some stay. Then the class session ends and it is time to go out and make plaster insects that can live in the tree.

On the whole, the class discussions and the way of working often take the form of a general discussion about things the children bring up. When a specific content that the teacher has planned is taken up, this is often characterised by a series of questions and answers, in which the children who already know the answers supply them. The class sessions usually last about 15 minutes. The most striking feature of the way of working is the long-term projects of a practical nature that the children work with. The teacher tries to follow the children, both in their associations in the class session and their suggestions about performing different activities, but does not try in a more purposeful way to direct children's thinking towards developing understanding. If anything, the philosophy appears to be that the children who are mature enough to assimilate something do so by constructing their own knowledge.

Preschool D

The teacher generally has a detailed plan, which means both that she has an area that is dealt with daily in class sessions, and that every day some table activity is linked up with what was discussed in the class session. They make many different things and do different kinds of exercises (perceptions, number, etc.) In addition to the exercises that everybody does after the class session, there is always a group that is "kept busy" with something the teacher has started off. A group of boys play, often noisily. As far as the organised activity is concerned, the teacher has generally prepared a model and copied it or cut out suitable pieces and generally taken out material designed to make it easier to produce "something". An example is when they have been talking about different conifers in the class session. Teacher sits down with four children at the table. She shows them how they cut out a piece of transparent sticky paper and fasten it to one side of a piece of card. You cut off a piece from each kind of tree (pine, juniper and spruce) and place it under the plastic film. The children follow suit but put the twigs in whatever order they like. Teacher has written the names of the different trees on her card. The children copy them down. One of them writes them in the same order as teacher, even though he has glued his twigs in a different order, he imitates without thinking himself. The exercises at the table which take up the theme of the class session often have the character of following instructions, in so far as the children get an instruction, which they carry out before teacher gives them the next one, etc. One example is when the children are to make figures for their clocks. They all receive a piece of squared paper, which teacher has divided into 12 large squares. A model is placed in front of the children. One child says she has done it to 13, but it is up to 12, only the two in 12 is back to front. When they have drawn their figures, they may cut them out. Someone asks, "What shall I do now?" Teacher says he can glue them onto the clock (a paper plate). Someone takes the initiative himself and cuts out the hands (teacher does this for the others) and also fastens them on.

On another occasion the children are to make roses (that unfold in water). Someone asks, "Haven't you done a model?" Teacher: "No, you can do what you like, as long as you can fold it." Teacher draws a star on the blackboard for the children to look at if they want. "I can't," says one. "Then it's good for you to practise," says teacher. Another child who can't says she doesn't want to do this kind of rose. "I'll do a drawing instead." Someone else asks teacher to draw. One can speculate about the children who say they can't. Do they do this because the task is too difficult or do they do it because they are accustomed to having a model or a teacher who helps them? I am inclined to believe that the latter is to blame, that is, the children are used to copying and using models and, therefore, cannot think independently either when engaged in such activities.

How can the class sessions be characterised then? The teacher has carefully prepared what she is going to say about the different things they take up. Generally the class session begins with the children being allowed to talk about what has happened to them for a short while. Presently the teacher interrupts by taking up the song "Hello children all...." Then the teacher begins speaking, and says "How we are going to talk about ..." The example I have chosen concerns the ladybird. The teacher holds up a picture of a ladybird and the children have to say what it is, is it a reptile or a ......" A child shouts, "A flying animal!" "It's a beetle," says teacher. She continues, "You can see that this ladybird is red, but there are others, too." "Yellow!, "Black!", "Orange!", the children call out. "I've seen..." and they talk about the different ladybirds they have seen. Teacher tells them that the spots can vary in colour and the ladybird has six legs. The red things at her sides are protective shields. Underneath them are the wings, so that she can fly, "It's poisonous," someone calls out.. But teacher goes on to say that the female ladybird lays lots of eggs early in the spring. The children joke about them looking like teeth and that it looks like an upper jaw. Teacher continues: "The female, she is so clever that she lays her eggs on a leaf which has something on it... what should there be?" "Greenfly," someone answers. "Yes, exactly. Greenfly is the main food of the ladybird. She lives on them, After a little while the eggs hatch and then the caterpillars crawl out and begin eating the greenfly. They live right in the middle of the larder, so they only have to help themselves and eat." The children laugh. Teacher goes on and says they eat till they are big and fat, that they spin themselves into a pupa and it takes 3 weeks from the egg stage to the finished ladybird. "I wouldn't like to be a ladybird," says one. "Neither would I." Teacher begins talking about the spots on the ladybird and that people usuallly say that the ladybird is as old as the number of spots, but that this is not true. They are born with a certain number of spots and they do not change. They go on to talk about the red colour, which is also a warning colour in traffic. Some animals eats ladybirds. But do you know what the ladybird does when it feels threatened? Well, it pretends to be dead, and lies there with its legs quite still. A yellow fluid comes out at the back of its knees which is poisonous. Teacher then goes on to talk about the origin of the Swedish name for ladybird, which is connected with the Virgin Mary and the fact that she used to carry a bunch of seven keys around with her. The sacred number is seven, sometimes you can see a candlestick with seven branches in church. And the ladybird often has.... how many spots?" "Seven," someone calls out. "Yes, that's why they call it "nyckelpiga" (literally "key maid"). She repeats the rhyme they used to say about the ladybird and what people say nowadays. Then she tells them that the weather will be fine if the ladybird flies away from your hand. The ladybird is a useful animal in that it eats up greenfly, because the greenfly eat up the leaves on our plants. Teacher goes on to say how the ladybird spends the winter in lichens and mosses. The class session ends with making a food chain with the leaf, the greenfly, the ladybird. Who eats the ladybird? "Birds" someone calls out. "And who catches the birds?" "The cat." "The dog". "But dogs don't eat cats, do they?" says teacher. She talks about birds of prey and reminds them that they are called animals of prey. "When it's dead, it turns to earth!" "Now we can see the whole circle, how it goes round." No-one has anything to ask about, but the children go on talking about Liseberg (Gothenburg's amusement park) and the "upside-down house" and then teacher thinks that it is enough for today.

All the children take part in the class sessions. There is a clear message that the teacher wishes to convey to them. She talks to them. Sometimes children try to say something, but there is not much time for this in the class session at least. These sessions last for about 20-25 minutes. The children carry out the planned activities all at the same time or in smaller groups (several at a time).

To sum up, one can say that teachers A and B work according to Figure 1 below, which means that they create situations and events where children have to reflect on both the content, the structure and their own learning, as well as on how they think at the different levels. Sometimes it is a question of moving from the specific to the more general and sometimes the reverse. On certain occasions attention is focussed naturally on all three levels, sometimes it is only on one level, fixing on the next level on another occasion.

1. The content -> Metacognition

2. The structure-> Metacognition

3. Learning-> Metacognition

Figure 1. The basis for the work in groups A and B

Since their own experience is taken as the point of departure and situations are created on which they can reflect, and thanks to their teachers' clear ideas about what they want to develop in their pupils in the way of understanding, these children are expected to learn in another way than in the other groups. Teacher C gives the impression of having a view of child development that implies that they should hear about certain facts, which will then be assimilated by the children who are mature enough for them. Teacher D has a more traditional view of learning as something that is transmitted and therefore presents the children with masses of facts. Both C and D's view of knowledge seems to be that the children must be taught facts first and that understanding will then grow out of these. In the C and D groups they assume that knowledge of facts must come first, while the A and B teachers try to work according to the principle that understanding comes first and is the foundation on which children can build other knowledge.

PART 3. RESULTS

The type of research results that will be reported here is based on the idea that it is the whole, that is, the pattern formed by all the results, that is essential. Despite this, different parts of the results will be reported separately. This is necessary because each result is associated with a specific method and purpose. The number of children in the various parts also varies somewhat, owing to the fact that four different groups were required to take part in the learning experiments and had to be interviewed at the same time (with one or two days in between). It was therefore impossible to return and follow up children who had been absent on some occasion during the research period. The long period over which data were collected, the wide variety of things studied, the rather large number of children who took part and my own involvement in developing work in the two experimental groups - all these factors have meant that no part of the report of the results can be seen in isolation. On the contrary, each part of the results must be seen in relation to other parts and to the theoretical starting-point, which is one of education, whose purpose is not only to increase our knowledge of how children develop understanding but to improve preschool didactics. In the tables, the children's answers have been placed in hierarchical order, that is, some have been assessed as more advanced than others.

4. CHILDREN'S CONCEPTIONS OF LEARNING IN PRESCHOOL

To discover whether or how children's awareness of their own learning is developed during the year in preschool, the children were interviewed on two occasions. The first one already took place within one or two weeks of starting the autumn term, when the children were assumed to have settled into the routines, and the other took place in the last week of the spring term. The main questions on both occasions were "Tell me about something you have learnt in preschool" and, referring to the child's example, "How did you go about learning that?" On the first occasion children were also asked "Do you think you are going to learn something in preschool. If so, what?"

Use is made here of the categories already described (see page 15), distinguishing children's conceptions of <u>what</u> they have learnt and <u>how</u> they have perceived learning comes about. Since these qualitatively different conceptions have been described in detail elsewhere (Pramling, 1983a), the following section will deal mainly with <u>quantitative</u> aspects, that is, interest will be focused on the frequency of the various conceptions among the children. The children's answers have been placed in hierarchical order in the sense that children who have expressed that they have learnt to know have not been indicated in the category "to do" because the latter is considered to be less advanced than the category "to learn to know". Earlier studies have shown that there is a developmental trend from the stage when children perceive that they learn to <u>do</u> things to one where they perceive that they learn to <u>know</u> things, and finally to one where they perceive that they learn to <u>understand</u> things.

4.1 What children think they have learnt

In Table 5 we can see how children's conceptions of learning are expressed in their answers about what they have learnt in preschool. The majority of children already have an idea about something they have learnt after they have been in preschool a few weeks. What they perceive they have learnt is to <u>do</u> something. In several of the groups the activities that predominate are weaving and sewing. But children also express that they have learnt to draw, play games, bake, sing songs, build, count, say children's names, write their names, not to draw outside the line, etc. Another form of activity that is expressed to some extent is that they have learnt to behave in a certain way, such as not to run indoors, not to go out in the playground without first asking teacher, not to quarrel, etc. The picture is somewhat different after a year in preschool. Now three-quarters of the children in group A and half of them in group B express that they have learnt to <u>know</u> about something. In the C group only one child (the same one as at the first interview) and in the D group five children give examples of something they have learnt to know. Two children are missing in group D. Thus, a change has taken place in three of the groups and it is especially noticeable in group A. Learning to know is expressed in the children's statements by their talking about the different themes they have worked with, for instance, that butterflies have four wings, about the life of animals in the woods, about mushrooms, etc. Several of the children in group A also indicate that they perceive that they have learnt to understand, which is expressed in their statements in that they talk about having learnt why it rains, about how bees make honey or about how the water from the sea evaporates to form rain.

Table 5. <u>Children's conceptions of what they have learnt in preschool just</u>
<u>after the start (1) and at the end (2) of the school year</u>

	Preschool							
	A		B		C		D	
Occasion	1	2	1	2	1	2	1	2
To do	16	4	18	11	17	16	13	10
To know	2	11	-	9	1	1	1	5
To understand	-	3	-	-	-	-	-	-
Don't know	1	1	2	-	2	3	1	-
No of children	19	19	20	20	20	20	15	15

The only children categorised in this table are ones that were present for both interviews, which explains why the number of children does not correspond to that given in Table 3. Two of the children in group C were interviewed about learning at the beginning of the spring term, having just arrived then. Four interviews from the first occasion are excluded for D group as the children concerned were absent on the second occasion. Of these four two have left and one child says she doesn't know. The remaining child perceives that she has learnt to do something.

As may be seen in Figure 2, the change in the experimental groups (A and B) is marked in comparison with the control groups. Groups A and B and groups C and D are combined in this diagram.

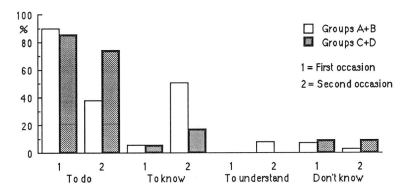

Figure 2. Block diagram to show the change in the experimental and control groups

The inter-judge reliability is 89%, which means that a judge put the children's answers in the same categories as the author to this extent.

At the first interview the children were also asked about what they thought they would learn in preschool during the year. As we see in Table 6, more than half the children in all groups do not know if they will learn anything or what they will learn. Among the children who have an idea about what they will learn, nearly all say that they will learn to do something.

Table 6. <u>What children think they will learn in preschool</u>

	Preschool			
	A	B	C	D
Don't know what or if	11	11	10	10
To do	6	9	8	8
To know	2	-	-	1
No of children	19	20	18	19

It is naturally difficult for children to be asked what they think they will learn. It means that they have to imagine something they have no experience of, but the same applies to the children in all the groups. What is interesting is that there is no difference between the groups. Either they have no idea or they think they will learn to draw, weave, play games, etc. What is puzzling about the children's answers is that in some of the groups many of the children had already attended preschool for one year, while in others a few had done so (see page 29). Consequently, these children should have answered differently from the others who had not attended before, but this was not the case.

4.2 Children's ideas of how they have learnt something

We can see from Table 7 <u>how</u> children think they have learnt to <u>do</u> something. This has either come about by someone showing them or talking about what they should do or by their carrying out the action or activity themselves. The only conceptions categorised in this table are the ones where children have expressed they have learnt to do something, meaning that those expressing that they have learnt to know or that they do not know what they have learnt at both interviews are excluded. On both occasions it is mostly children in group C who perceive that they have learnt to do something by doing it themselves. Otherwise, the main difference between the groups is that fewer children from groups A and B only have the idea that they have only learnt to do something. Two children express the idea that they learnt to do something by thinking it out.

Table 7. Children's conceptions of how they have learnt to do something

	Preschool							
	A		B		C		D	
Occasion	1	2	1	2	1	2	1	2
By doing	8	3	9	6	13	14	5	8
By being told or shown	7	-	9	5	3	2	8	2
By thinking	1	1	-	-	1	-	-	-
No of children	16	4	18	11	17	16	13	10

The numbers in Table 7 only refer to those children in each group who perceived that they had learnt to do something, which accounts for the smaller number of children on the second occasion.

As we saw in Table 5, on the first occasion children rarely expressed that they had learnt to know anything. Only a few children's ideas about how they learned to know are therefore shown for the first occasion in Table 8. On the second occasion, the greatest difference lies between the A and B groups, on the one hand, in which development takes place, and the C and D groups, on the other, where the change is only marginal. A large proportion of the children in group A embrace the idea that you can learn to know as a result of your own activities, but only three children in group B do so. Two children in group A have developed an idea that you can learn to know by thinking.

Table 8. Children's conceptions of how they have learnt to know

					Preschool			
	A		B		C		D	
Occasion	1	2	1	2	1	2	1	2
External influence	-	-	-	6	1	1	1	5
Their own activity	2	12	-	3	-	-	-	-
By thinking	-	2	-	-	-	-	-	
No of children	2	14	0	9	1	1	1	5

In conclusion, one can say that there is a marked difference between the A and B groups and the C and D groups in that the children in the first two groups have developed a greater awareness of their own learning than those in the other two. Comparison of groups A and B shows that group A have developed their conceptions most, while comparison of groups C and D shows that more children have developed in group D. In both the experimental groups, but most obviously in group A, the metacognitive dialogues about what things they have done in preschool and how and why they did them appear to have developed children's awareness not only of what they have learnt but of how this has come about.

4.3 Children's ideas about why they visited the Natural History Museum

During the last few days at preschool the children's own teacher interviewed them, and one of the questions she asked was, "Why did Ingrid take you to the Natural History Museum ?" The latter was included in one of the teaching experiments during the spring term (see page 84).

Clear qualitative differences in the children's conceptions appeared, which after they were described and placed in hierarchical order showed that some children had realised that they had visited the museum to learn something, meaning that they had seen through the purpose of the visit. Other children talk instead about going to look at animals (some child says listen to something about animals). These children never make the connection between themselves and their learning, but the visit to the Natural History Museum is regarded as just like any other activity, something that you just do. A few children say it was because it's <u>fun</u>, that is, they are not just doing something, they are doing it for fun.

Table 9. <u>The purpose of the visit to the Natural History Museum</u>

	Preschool			
	A	B	C	D
To learn	19	13	5	7
Look at (hear about) animals	-	5	10	5
For fun	-	1	-	1
Don't know	-	2	3	4
No of children	19	21	18	17

We see in Table 9 that all the children in the A group appear to have understood that they were taken to the museum to learn something. Just over half the children in the B group realised this, while barely a third of those in the C group and just over a third of those in the D group did so.On child said, "It was just so she could interview us and see if we had learnt anything there".

4.4 Discussion

The A group appear to have an awareness of learning that is far superior to that in all the other groups, not only when faced with a direct question about what and why they have learnt, but also when asked why they had to go to the Natural History Museum. About half the children in the B group have developed an awareness that you can learn to know things during their year at preschool, but this insight is only found among a quarter of the children in D group and in only one child in the C group. As far as the relation between those who see their learning as the result of external influence and those who see it as the result of their own activity is concerned, only a few children in the B group have understood that they can learn to know by being active themselves, while more than half of those in the A group have done so. In the A group all the children have understood that the reason for visiting the Natural History Museum was to learn something, while in the B group just over half the children have realised this. This insight is much less common among the children in the C and D groups.

There is every indication that the way of working in the A and B groups, that is, getting the children to reflect on their own learning in the form of what they have done during the year and how and why they have done it, has led to the development of a greater degree of awareness of their own learning. This method of thematising the learning aspect and getting children to reflect on how they think about learning was used earlier in another group of children to develop their conceptions of what they learn and how this comes about (see page 16). It seems, therefore, that this way of working to develop children's conceptions of their own learning functions in different types of group.

5. THE STORY ABOUT THE RED APPLE

The first learning experiment was based on how children understand "The story about the red apple" by J. Lööf. It was conducted by an assistant preschool teacher who had experience of children through her own work and of interviewing children through the courses she was attending. The assistant teacher had only been informed that I was working in different ways at the different preschools, but knew nothing of what was going on at any particular preschool. The results of the learning experiment with "The story about the red apple", which will be described here, should be seen in the light of the fact that it also provided the assistant with her first opportunity of getting to know the children, since she also took part in another learning experiment (the cycle) later on.

5.1 How the learning experiment was carried out

To carry out the learning experiment the assistant teacher read the story to the whole group, showing the pictures at the same time. After this the children were allowed to make a drawing. The main reason for this was that the children would then have something concrete with them when they later went into an adjoining room to be interviewed by the assistant.

This story was chosen because it had a structure in the form of a relationship in which one event led to another, something that no group had specifically worked with previously.

The story is about two apples that are exchanged. An old man goes to a fruit shop to buy an apple. The fruit-dealer plays a joke on the old man and gives him a green apple, which he is told to take home with him and put on the window-sill to ripen. However, the apple is made of plastic. In the fruit-dealer's garden hangs a beautiful big red apple that he intends to enter for a competition. The old man goes home and <u>places the apple in the window</u> while he gets down to bulding a model. Meanwhile the old man's parrot comes and <u>knocks down</u> the apple so that it lands on the head of old granny, sitting outside. <u>Granny screams</u> and frightens the cat so much that it runs up a tree. <u>A boy</u> who is passing by <u>gets the blame</u> for the apple falling on granny's head. In tears, he runs off right in front of the headmaster's car. <u>The headmaster</u> has to brake suddenly and <u>then drives straight into the fruit -dealer's fence</u>. While the headmaster and the fruit-dealer are quarrelling with each other, <u>another boy</u> takes the opportunity to creep in through the hole that has appeared in the fence and <u>take the fruit-dealer's red apple</u>. The boy intends to give it to his teacher at school so as to get better marks. However, there is chaos <u>in the classroom</u> because all the children are looking out of the window at the policeman who is looking for a <u>robber</u>, so the teacher doesn't take any notice of the apple. The robber is hiding behind a wall chart of a human being. He runs forward and takes the apple with him on his way out. In the corridor <u>the robber bumps into the headmaster</u> so that he drops the apple, which flies out through the window. <u>It is caught by a fireman</u>, who is on his way to granny's to get her cat down. The fireman takes a bite out of the apple and then puts it down <u>on the man's window-sill</u> while he climbs up to get the cat. <u>The old man discovers that the apple has ripened</u>, but scolds his parrot because he thinks it's the bird that has taken a bite out of it. Later on the old man goes to the fruit-dealer and thanks him for the the nice apple he had bought from him. Then the fruit-dealer sees that his apple is missing, but cannot understand how this happened.

The children were asked to talk about their drawing and then to say what the story was about. "What happened next?" "What did the old man do then?" The children have thus been prompted a little so that they can go on with the story.

5.2 Result of the first learning experiment

Since "The story about the red apple" is both common and popular, the children were asked if they had heard it before. It was then shown that most of the children had already encountered it. The groups differ somewhat as to the number of children who stated they had heard it earlier. Only one child in group D stated that he had not heard before, while a quarter of the children in groups A and B said they had not heard it previously. Finally, in group C about half the children appear not to have heard the story before.

As far as the children's drawings are concerned, most contain a picture of an apple, although in different connections. Some children draw only the apple(s), others a tree with an apple, an apple on the window-sill, granny being hit on the head with the apple, the old man and the apple, the fire-engine, the headmaster who had a collision with his car, and the shop. The most common motive is the apple hanging in the tree. No appreciable difference was seen between the groups.

It is very difficult to analyse the children's interviews on the basis of how they have understood the story, partly because most of the children tell what happened in the story in chronological order, partly because there so many stages in the story that many children find it hard to remember it and go on retelling it without a certain amount of prompting. The children's natural way of telling such a story in the form of first <u>this</u> happened and then <u>that</u>, etc., has also been used and stimulated by the interviewer, who said to the children that couldn't get started, "Once there was an old man who went to the fruit shop and bought an apple ... what happened next?" <u>A few</u> children start off their story with the two apples being exchanged, but when asked how this happened they go on to tell the whole story. Because so few children start off with both apples, there is no point in analysing the children's statements according to whether the children do or do not have the two apples as their starting-point. Instead, I have decided to analyse the interviews in the traditional manner, on the basis of how many events in the story the children succeed in producing, with a certain amount of help or without any at all. The interviewer's help is accepted if she takes hold of what the child has said and asks what happened next (e.g. What did the boy do with the apple then?" or "How did the teacher like getting an apple from Bert?" or "How did the apple get back on the old man's window-sill?"). The children's statements are no longer counted if the interviewer herself has told part of the story in order to get the child to continue.

The 11 main events in the story on which the analysis is based are marked in the summary of the story on page 63. The children's answers have been categorised according to the number of events they have included: 8-11 , 5-7, 2-4 events or only 1 event. Let us look at a few examples from the different categories.

5.2.1 Retold 8-11 events in the story

The children in this category have not only succeeded in including many events but also seem to have understood that it is a question of two different apples and how the actual exchnage took place.

Lisa: The old man had bought an apple, then he got a funny apple. Then he was supposed to put it in the window, then he worked on his model boat and put it together. And he had a parrot who happened to poke it so it fell down on granny who sat underneath on the first floor. Then a boy went past and she thought that it was he who had thrown the apple, so she was angry with him. Then he ran right out into the street and didn't look where he was going, then the headmaster came with his new car, then he swerved so as not to run over him then he drove right into the fence where the man had the apple. Then a boy came who was cycling to school and he saw the apple and took it to give to his teacher. But she didn't see the apple because she was only looking at the policeman who stood outside the window and asked if they had seen a man in a false beard and sunglasses.Then he stood behind the map, but while they were looking the robber came out and took the apple and went. But then he happened to run right into the headmaster and dropped the apple right through the window. Then the fire brigade came to get a cat out of the tree, then the fireman caught the apple in his hand and took a bite. He couldn't have his hands full of things and fetch a cat down, so when he climbed up he put it on the window-sill where the old man sat. So when the old man was ready with his boat he saw the apple was red and thought it had turned red while he stood there. Then he saw there was a bite (out of it). Then he was cross with the parrot because he thought it was him though it was the fireman. Then he want out and ate his apple. Then he went to the fruit-dealer and told him what a lovely apple that he had given him.

Emma: It was about an old man who was given an apple made of plastic. The man in the shop played a trick on him (and said) that if he put it in the sunshine it would get ripe.

Interviewer: Can it ripen?

Emma: Oh, no, but he put it in the window at home. But his parrot knocked it down, so it landed on granny's head and she got angry and thought it was Per, a little boy who did it. He was upset because he hadn't been naughty, then a boy called Bertil came and was going to give a red apple that the fruit-dealer had to his teacher, so he'd get better marks, he thought. Then there was a robber in the classroom who took the apple. Then Bertil told the policeman that the robber was standing outside the window. When the robber took the apple away he bumped into the headmaster in the corridor, then he dropped the apple and then the "firebrigademan" caught the apple. Then when he had to take a cat down from the tree he put the apple on the window ledge where the old man lived and then the old man took the apple and told the parrot that he was not allowed to bite it.

5.2.2 Retold 5-7 events in the story

It cannot be said that the children assigned to this category have generally understood that there were two apples and how they were exchanged, but many of the children have realised this.

Mathias: He went to a fruit shop and bought an artificial apple and when he went home he began to build his model aeroplane, then the parrot happened to knock the apple so that it fell on old granny's head, and her kitten ran up a tree. Then the fireman came to get the cat down and then he found the lovely apple which fell down and took it and put it on his window-ledge and said "What a lovely apple," although he thought the parrot had taken a bite out of the apple and scolded the parrot..

Ann-Charlotte: It was the green apple that he didn't know was a plastic apple. Then he got it and put it on the window-sill, then he sat and painted something on his model boat. Then the parrot came and knocked down the apple onto old granny and then Per was sad just because she thought that he was the one who threw the apple and..don't remember exactly.

Interviewer: How was the old man able to get the real apple in the end?

Ann-Charlotte: Just because the fire-brigade put it on the window-sill.

5.2.3 Retelling of 2-4 events in the story

The children in this category often seem to have little idea of how it all happened if they have at all understood that two apples were involved.

Jonas: He got a plastic apple instead and he put it in the window so that it would ripen, but it was only a plastic apple, of course..but then he got a real apple.

Interviewer: But how was he able to get the real apple then?

Jonas: Well, I don't know.

Stig: The headmaster had a car crash and the apple that hit the old lady on the head, then she thought it was that boy who went past.. and began to make a fuss and then.. well, then I don't know all of it.

Henrik: Yes, about a robber who took the apple that flew in through the window..it was the headmaster he bumped into.

Interviewer: Was it the headmaster who took the apple?

Henrik: No, it flew out through the window in the school.

Interviewer: How did the old man in the striped suit get the apple then?

Henrik: He went to a fruit shop and bought it.

Linnea: He bought a plastic apple and the parrot pushed it so that it fell out of the window.. don't remember everything.

Interviewer: Did the old man get a real apple in the end or did he still have his plastic apple?

Linnea: .Yes, he still had it, I suppose, but I'm not sure.

5.2.4 Only retold one event

The children placed in this category generally only know that the story was about an apple, or they have completely erroneous ideas.

Marcus: The old man bought an apple, but it was made of plastic.

Interviewer: Did he want a plastic apple?

Marcus: No, not really..

Interviewer: Why did he get a plastic apple?

Marcus: I don't know..

Interviewer: When the book was finished and the old man went to town with the apple, was it a plastic apple then too?

Marcus: No, it was real..

Interviewer: How could he have got a real one in the end, then?

Marcus: Just because it lay in the sun.

Lars: An old man and a parrot and a boy.

Interviewer: What did they do then?

Lars: Went into a shop and bought things..apples..then he drove into it with his car, then the thief ate up everything.

Interviewer: Where was the apple?

Lars: For the cat.

Interviewer: Did the cat take the apple?

Lars: Yes.

Wilhelm: About the red apple.

Interviewer: What happened to the red apple?

Wilhelm: ...don't remember.

Although the children were given numerous clues, they did not succeed in explaining very much about what happened in the story.

5.2.5 The number of events retold in the different groups

We can see in Table 10 how the answers from the different preschools are divided, that is, how many events they succeeded in retelling.

Table 10. <u>The number of events in the story that were retold</u>

	Preschool			
	A	B	C	D
8 - 11 events	10	7	-	3
5 - 7 events	5	5	5	1
2 - 4 eventsl	2	8	8	12
1 event	-	1	6	1
No of children	17	21	19	17

The Chi^2 test shows a significant difference between the experimental and the control groups (X^2= 18.2; <u>df</u>=3;p. <.001). We can also see in the table that in group A more that half the children retell so many events in the story that one can assume that they have understood how the exchange took place. In the B group about a third of the children have retold most events in the story. In the D group only a few children and in the C group no child did so. The C group is also the group in which most children did not succeed in explaining what happened in the story at all. There was agreement between the judges as regards 93% of the answers.

If the experimental and control groups are compared with regard to how large a proportion of the children have retold 5 events or more, nearly all those in group A fall and somewhat half of those in group B fall within this category. In contrast, only a quarter of the children in groups C and D retell this number of events. Figure 3 also illustrates the differences after the experimental groups, on the one hand, and the control groups, on the other, were combined.

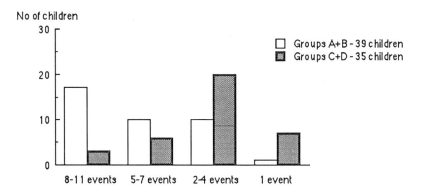

Figure 3. Block diagram showing the differences between the experimental and control groups regarding the number of events in the story that were retold.

5.3 Discussion

When the story was selected I thought there was a clear connection between the various stages in the story about how the apple was exchanged and then went from person to person (and event). When one examines the children's statements, one can see that there are too many events for the connection to be clearly understood. Nevertheless, a fair number of children have succeeded in including most of the events when retelling the story. Zirisky (1986) has shown in one study that when children aged 6 - 10 years (primary school) are required to give a free rendering of a text they have read, they tend to reproduce rather than interpret it.

The story is a difficult one, making it conceivable that children who have heard it before have an advantage and can remember a number of events more easily. Only half the children in the C group have heard the story previously. It is also shown that no child completely grasps the story and that a third have not succeeded at all in expressing what the story was about so that it is obvious that they have understood anything at all. The assumption that it is easier to understand if one has heard the story before was not borne out by the children in group D, nearly all of whom have heard it before (have read it in preschool). Yet very few are able to retell the story to any great extent. It seems quite simply that the children in the groups (A and B) where they have worked with the special didactic approach involving an alternation between different levels of generality (where the children have reflected on relations at one level) have found it easier to perceive the structure in the story than the children in the other groups have. Neither of the experimental groups, however, have worked with the particular structure to be found in this story.

6. THE STORY: THE OTHER SIDE OF THE RIVER

The second learning experiment also consisted of finding out whether and how children understand the message in a story, one with a clear structure in the form of cause and effect, that is, seeing the author's point meant that the children had to understand that the people are mutually dependent on each other.

The story "On the other side of the river" is neither Swedish nor very well known, which means that no child had heard it earlier. It concerns a village (Hagaby on the river), which lies on both sides of a river. The river is crossed by an old bridge. The people on the east bank are quarrelling with the people on the west bank. One stormy night the bridge is blown down and the people on both sides are pleased because they won't be troubled by the people on the other side, until one day the baker finds that his buns are covered in soot and he has to ring for the chimney sweep to come and sweep his chimney. But, oh no, he lives on the other side of the river. Another day the blacksmith has an accident with his sledgehammer and needs to seek a doctor. But that's not possible either, because he's on the other side of the river. This theme is repeated over and over again. One evening people set off rowing from either side of the river. The boats meet out on the water and people fall in when they try to climb into each other's boats. So they decide to build a new bridge, and this is done. At the end of the story all is harmony and concord.

6.1 How the learning experiment was carried out

When the children had heard the story without having seen the pictures or being told its name, they were asked to draw something to do with the story.

After that they were interviewed individually. First the children were required to talk about their drawings, which automatically led many of them into the action of the story. "Tell me something more about the story." When the children did not seem to be able to say anything more about the story without clues, they were asked questions about central and critical elements. "Who lived in the village?" "What happened to the bridge?" "Why did it fall down?" "What happened then?" "Why did they build a new bridge?" All the questions were then followed up according to what the children said. The interview ended with the children being given the task of thinking up a name for the story. I have read the story and interviewed the children in all the groups.

6.2 Results of the second learning experiment

6.2.1 The children's drawings

Let us first look at what children draw when they do not have any experience in the form of visual impressions but only pictures they have formed in their own minds. (Certainly, it is true here as in similar situations that some children glance furtively at their neighbour's efforts to get a start). As we see in Table 11, the most usual drawing is of a river with a bridge over it (in about half of these drawings there were also houses). To almost the same extent, children then draw different occupations and boats with or without people in them. One child draws people swimming and some children only draw houses.

Table 11. Children's drawings about "The other side of the river"

	Preschool			
	A	B	C	D
River and bridge	11	14	11	12
Different occupations	5	2	2	1
Boats and water	1	4	5	1
Houses	-	1	2	3
Someone swimming	1	-	-	-
No of children	18	21	20	17

The table shows that there is practically no difference between the groups as regards the subjects of their drawings. In other words, the distribution of the children's conceptions of what the story is about is similar in all groups. About half the children bear in the mind the essential things in the story, the river and the bridge. The other children take up things that have a less prominent place. As far as drawing conclusions from the children's drawings is concerned, one should probably be cautious. It is also possible, of course, that the river and the bridge were the easiest things to draw. Those who drew different occupations or something else may also be perfectly well aware of the point. As regards the interpretation of drawings, one can never ignore the children's skill in representing things graphically (Goodnow, 1985).

6.2.2 Giving the story a name

Most of the children give the story a title that is connected with something in the plot of the story, a situation or a person in it, such as "The bridge that fell down", "The land of the troublemakers", "The story of the shoemaker" (farmer, chimney-sweep, baker) etc. One child said: "It's probably called *The other side of the river*, that is, the same title the author had given it. Another group of children give answers that are not directly connected with the action, such as "Nisse", "Pippi", "Doctor Snuggles", etc (there are no persons with such names) or very general names, such as "The exciting story", "The crazy-makers" (from a popular group of comedians), that is, names that can be regarded as <u>irrelevant</u>. The distribution of the children who thought of titles connected with the plot of the story and those who didn't, and also those who couldn't think of anything, can be seen in Table 12.

Table 12. <u>What kind of name the children give the story</u>

| | Preschool | | | |
	A	B	C	D
Connected with plot	16	18	10	7
Irrelevant	-	1	7	5
Don't know	2	2	3	4
No of children	18	21	20	17

Here there seems to be a certain difference between the A and B groups, on the one hand, and the C and D groups, on the other, as regards giving the story a relevant title or not. Can this be an indication of how the children in the different groups have understood the story. Let's see!

6.2.3 What the children say spontaneously about the plot

The children's spontaneous answers to the question "What is the story about" vary both as regards the content they take up and what they appear to have understood of the meaning. The qualitatively different ways of telling the story that can be distinguished are that some children understand the relation east-west as mutual dependence, while other children only appear to have understood a single section of the story.

Thus, some children focus on the <u>mutual dependence</u>, that is, the fact that the village consisted of two parts that could not function without depending on each other. If they didn't have a bridge, they couldn't get help from the ones living on the other side, and vice-versa.

Katrin: A bridge fell down and they used to quarrel all the time, so they thought it was good that the bridge fell down, but then they needed each other.

Sara: It was about a village that lay on both sides of a river..they quarrelled an awful lot, but then they found when their bridge was broken that they needed each other..there was only one baker, one chimney-sweep and one doctor, of course.

Other children make a mental note of only <u>one section</u> of the story. This can vary in content, such as the bridge fell down (or that they built a new one), the occupations, boats and water or quarrelling. Some children talk about several of these sections but do not connect them with the whole, that they they never mention the mutual dependence.

Johanna: That the bridge broke down.

Lars: He fell in and caught hold of the bridge,..yes, when he walked up and down then the chimney-sweep came and then he lost his boot.

Ann-Charlotte: That they fell into the water and swam to the bridge--Don't remember.

There is certainly a group of children, too, who cannot say what the story is about.

Table13. <u>What children say spontaneously about the plot of the story</u>

	Preschool			
	A	B	C	D
Mutual dependence	8	8	-	-
Some section	6	11	14	12
Don't know	4	2	6	5
No of children	18	21	20	17

The Chi^2 test shows a significance difference between the experimental groups and the control groups (X^2=19.3; df=2; p=<.001). As we also see in Table 13, the difference lies mainly between groups A and B, on the one hand, and groups C and D, on the other, as far as their ability to talk spontaneously about what the story was about. Both in group A and group B there are eight childen who bring out the main point of the story, while no child in the other groups does so.

6.2.4 Remembering details

One question the children were asked was: "Who lived in the village?" This can be regarded purely as a test of memory, in which the children have to remember and reproduce details and list as many as they can think of.

The individuals most children in all groups remember are the baker and the chimney-sweep. After that comes the tailor, who is sometimes called "the sewer". One can also see here that children make up new persons themselves, who were not mentioned in the story, such as the nurse, the gardener, the old ladies or the singer. When they were listing how many people they could remember from the story, there was no marked difference betweeen the groups. On average, the children in groups A, B and C could count up to just over three persons in the village per child, while the figure for the D group was just under three persons per child. In this respect then, remembering and naming individuals, there does not seem to be any appreciable difference between the groups.

6.2.5 Why did the bridge collapse?

The collapse of the bridge is, of course, a central happening in the story, while <u>how</u> this came about can be regarded as a detail. All the same, understanding why the bridge collapsed presupposes that the children perceive the relation between the <u>bad weather conditions</u> and the age of the bridge. Other children seem to have formed other relations, either on the basis of other events in the story, such as that the bridge fell down because the people <u>quarrelled</u>, or that the bridge collapsed because of some kind of <u>damage</u>. Some children cannot give any reason for the bridge falling down.

<u>Old bridge and bad weather</u>
Children who have understood the cause of the collapse of the bridge as it is described in the story refer to a storm, rain or thunder, that is, terrible weather. Sometimes they combine the bad weather with the fact that the bridge was old, and sometimes they talk of only one of these aspects.

Ted: It fell down in a storm.

Magdalena: Because it was so windy and there was thunder.

Andreas: Maybe it was old and rotten.

Cecilia: Only because they had walked on it and it was old, I think.

Quarrelling

Children who thought the bridge collapsed because of the quarrelling in the village are probably thinking of their own world, where adults sometimes say: "Stop fighting or it may break," as can happen when two children are tugging at the same thing.

Martina: I think it was because they quarrelled so much.

Damage

Some children seem to have imagined that a boat has crashed into the bridge or that it has been damaged by cars so that it has collapsed, that is, events not found in the story.

Pontus: Two boats that were too big went under it.

Anders: Perhaps it was broken.

Linda: Maybe someone drove into it.

Let's look at Table 14 to see how the various ideas about why the bridge collapsed are distributed within the different groups.

Table 14. Why the brdige collapsed according to the children

	Preschool			
	A	B	C	D
Old/bad weather	12	16	8	3
Quarrelling	1	1	1	1
Damage	2	-	5	2
Don't know	3	4	6	8
No of children	18	21	20	14(3)

For some unknown reason, three children in groups D did not get this question. Despite this, a marked difference may be seen between the A and B groups and the C and D groups regarding the reason for the collapse of the bridge. More than half the children in the A and B groups have understood the relationship that came out in the story, while only a minority of the children in the other groups have done so. A large proportion of the children in group D cannot think of any explanation.

6.2.6 Why was a new bridge built?

The question why they built a new bridge may be regarded as the most essential one in this learning experiment. The different conceptions that appeared about why the bridge was rebuilt were: that they <u>needed each other</u>, so that they would be able <u>get across</u>, and that they became <u>friends</u>, while some had no idea. The children who did not know sometimes invented something that was not in the story at all, such as, that the bridge was built to tie boats to or to go up on when you had been swimming.

<u>They needed each other</u>
This conception focuses on the message of the story, that is, the people on one side of the river are dependent on the people on the other side, and vice-versa.

Helena: Just so they could get across if they needed help.

Henrik: Because they needed each other.

Michael: Well, supposing they got ill, then they would have to be able to get over to the other side where the doctor was.

<u>To get across the river</u>
The reason for building a new bridge is to get across to the other side. Either the children cannot explain why the people want to cross over, or they say that the people on one side want to go and visit the people on the other side of the river.

Lisa: So they would be able to get across.

Lars: Other people would get across.

Became friends

The children have the idea that the reason for building a new bridge is the people on each side have become good friends again and, consequently, do not quarrel any more.

Kristina: Well, just because they became friends then.

Per: Because they were good again.

In Table 15 we can see how children's conceptions of why a new bridge was built are distributed among the different groups. The childen who said that the people wanted to get across the bridge or became friends were asked: "Why did they become good friends?" One child in the A group, three children in the B group and four in the C group (and none in group D) were then added to the category "needed each other".

Table 15. Children's conceptions of why a new bridge was built

	Preschool			
	A	B	C	D
Needed each other	16	13	10	2
To get across	1	2	1	6
Became friends	1	3	1	5
Don't know	-	3	8	3
No of children	18	21	20	17

The Chi^2 test shows a significance difference between the experimental groups and the control groups (X^2=11.2; df=3; p=<.02). The A group stands out as being far superior to the others. All but two of the children have realised that the bridge was built because the people needed each other or were dependent on each other. More than half the children in group B have understood this dependence, while about half those in group C have done so. The categories of the co-judge and the researcher coincided for 78% of the children's answers.

6.3 Discussion

The groups of children differ from each in certain respects, and not in others. When it is a question of creating a picture in the form of a drawing, as well as when the children have to list the people living in the village, there is no appreciable difference between one group and another. As regards questions directed towards an understanding of the situation, on the other hand, a clear difference can be seen between the two experimental groups (A and B) and the other two (C and D). At the very beginning, when asked to talk about the story, a large proportion of the children in groups A and B bring out its cardinal point , while not one child in the other groups does so. As far as the difference between group A and group B is concerned, more children in group A have realised what the author's message was, while comparison of groups C and D shows that more children in group C have understood that the people needed each other. The structure of this story can be said to refer to the relation of cause and effect, something which the children in group B worked with especially. Nevertheless, more children in group A understood this relation.

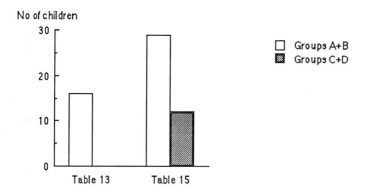

Figure 4.Block diagram to show the differences between the experimental groups (A + B) and the control groups (C + D) concerning the children's understanding of the mutual dependence as expressed in Tables 13 and 15.

The differences between the experimental and control groups are brought out clearly in Figure 4. One can also see that it is more difficult for children to focus on the point of the story when allowed to retell it in their own words (see Table 13) than when they are given a more specific questions (see Table 15). However, the differences between the groups remain, whatever the form of the question.

7. CHILDREN'S UNDERSTANDING OF AN ECOLOGICAL CYCLE

The purpose of the third learning experiment was to discover whether children were able to understand an ecological cycle when being taught about it. The reason for choosing a cycle was that, in order to understand it, children have to perceive the structure, that is, the relations forming a cycle. This is a structure that the A group has worked with in connection with other contents (e.g. in the theme "Rain and water", "The yearly cycle of the bee colony" and "The shop"). They have, however, not worked with the ecological cycle. One of the control groups (group D), on the other hand, have to a certain extent. They have studied different food chains, involving, for example, the ant, the earthworm and the spruce forest, though not as a closed cycle. Thus, group A has worked with the relational structure and group D with the content. In contrast, groups B and C have not worked specifically with either of these.

7.1 How the learning experiment was carried out

The lesson on the ecological cycle took place at the Natural History Museum. The project leader and the curator of the museum (Kalle) had conferred together on how to present the information to the children. One preschool group per day on four consecutive days was required to go to the museum to acquaint itself with Kalle's "lesson" about the cycle. The lesson was recorded both on tape and in note form in order to detect any differences that may have arisen during the different presentations.

The follow up in the form of interviews with the children was undertaken by an assistant (teacher) who did not know what had taken place in the different groups (see Methods, page 31). Before the interviews the children had to draw something that they remembered from the visit to the museum.

In the following interviews with each child in turn, they were first asked to talk about their drawings. This prompted some of the children to talk about what Kalle had said or done. If this didn't happen, they were asked: "What did Kalle talk to you about at the museum yesterday?" "Did he talk about anything else?" If the child had still not mentioned the cycle, it was asked: "Do you remember that Kalle put out all the things (soil, tree, insects, earthworm, bird) on the floor and drew arrows between them. Why did he do that?" "Do you remember what he called it?" "Why did he call it that?" The children who still did not show any sign of having understood the cycle were then given all the parts in the form of paper models and urged to tell a story about the pictures to a doll.

7.1.1 The lesson at the museum

The children came to the museum with their teacher. They had to hang up their outdoor clothes and look round the entrance hall while waiting for Kalle to come and fetch them. In the room where the lesson was given there were some stuffed birds on a shelf and a wolf. Otherwise the room was empty except for a ring of chairs on the floor.

In all the groups the lesson begins with Kalle bringing out a stuffed fieldfare. The children have to guess what kind of bird it is. Kalle tells them that it is also called a snow magpie. The also look at the blackbird and are then allowed to listen to different bird songs on tape. The talk a while about why birds sing. Kalle then takes out a "dead fieldfare" and the children have to reflect on why it has died and what happens to it when it is lying on the ground. The children talk about various dead birds they have seen. Their attention is drawn to the sexton beetles and other insects to be found round the dead fieldfare. Kalle talks about how the insects eat parts of the dead bird and how they then "do a number two", which turns into nourishment for the soil (turns into soil). They talk about the farmers spreading out cow manure on the fields and the children have to ponder over the things that want the food. Trees and flowers want nourishment! Then some green leaves are brought out and they talk about these turn into brown leaves in the autumn. "Who likes leaves?" wonders Kalle. The worms do, of course! The children are shown a little plastic box containing soil, leaves, live insects and earthworms. Then comes the last link in the chain. "Who eats worms?" Some child answers: "Birds" and the cycle is completed. Kalle has laid out the different parts one by one on the floor during the discussion.

Now he goes over them again by asking questions. At the same time he draws arrows on the floor between the various parts and informs them that it is called a <u>cycle</u>. He also explains why it is called a cycle and they go over it again in various ways.

This is the main message that is conveyed to all groups, and it takes about 45 minutes in all. The talk about every part of the cycle that Kalle introduces and also about the things the children associate with it.

The difference that can be seen between the groups, besides some deviation from the content as regards individual components, is that, in the D group, special emphasis was laid on what happens if some component of the cycle disappears. In the A group Kalle put the parts in a semi-circle and called it a food chain. He did not notice this until the project leader pointed it out to him, and then he rearranged the parts to form a cycle. The last lesson was given to the C group. It was also the best one in that the structure of the cycle was brought out most clearly here.

7.2 Results of the third learning experiment

It is impossible to discover from their drawings whether the children realised that the purpose of the visit to the museum was to learn something, as the task they were given was to draw something they remembered seeing there. They were thus free to draw things from outside the room where the lesson was held. We can see in Table 16 that much of what the children drew was not included in the lesson.

Table 16. <u>The children's drawings after visiting the museum</u>

	Preschool			
	A	B	C	D
From the entrance hall	6	14	5	-
Something in the cycle	6	2	6	13
Stuffed animals	4	3	7	4
The children	3	-	-	-
Antal barn	19	19	18	17

What attracted the attention of the children in the entrance hall of the museum were the bears, wall charts of dinosaurs and "The most dangerous animal in the world - man". The B group especially had to wait in the entrance hall for some time and then showed great interest in the dinosaurs. They were something the children had already shown in interest in before at preschool. Some of them had brought books about these animals to preschool. The D group had the shortest time to wait in the entrance hall and did not notice anything there either. It is this group, on the other hand, that have most often drawn something from the cycle. Most of the drawings of the stuffed animals in the classroom (the wolf or a cock) were done by the children in group C. Three children from the A group did drawings of the other children, either sitting in a ring during the lesson or waiting outside the museum. As before, it is not without relevance, of course, that when children draw they glance at or copy each other's efforts.

7.2.1 Children's conceptions of the cycle

Analysis of the children's answers to the question what Kalle had talked to them about at the musuem shows that four different levels of understanding can be distinguished. First there are children who have understood the relation in the form of a <u>cycle</u>. At the next level, children can link up several relations in the form of a <u>food chain</u>. The third level comprises children who have understood some <u>fragment</u> of the food chain. Finally, there are the children who only <u>give a name to</u> something from the lesson.

The cycle

This category comprises the children who have understood the whole, that is, how all the parts depend on each other for nutrition. They close the chain, so to speak, to form a cycle.

Viktor: He told us all that about birds and worms, that a bird lived a few years and then died, of course, and then the insects and beetles came and ate out of it. Then the sextons come and bury it, then they "pooh" and it turns into soil and then the plants like the soil and they take it and grow. Then they lose their leaves in the autumn, and the worms come and eat up the leaves. Then there were leaf sparrows - or leaf mapgie or something, then the plants would grow a few years, then they would die from lack of food and lost a lot of leaves and the worms were gone, then they just lay there.

Lisa: It's that cycle, there are two birds, one's called the brown one, a female that's a blackbird, the other's a fieldfare. Then they die and maybe insects come and eat it up, then it turns into soil. Then the trees grow out of the soil. Then the leaves come too and the worms like the leaves lying in piles, but then the birds eat up the worm.

The food chain

The children's conceptions in this category express that they understand that certain parts supply food for some other part, that is, some relations that are obvious to the children. They do not, however, conceive the complete cycle.

Ted: That bird lived till it was five, then it died. Then lots of insects came and then the beetle came and buried it. Then it lay eggs inside it. Then the grubs ate up the bird, then they pooed it out. Then it turned into soil.

Interviewer: Then what happened to the soil?

Ted: The plants needed it. Then it grew up and then it faded and then the worm came and ate it all up.

Peter: He talked about animals. That a food chain, that animals died and live sort of, and first a bird, then the insects come and eat it up, then it turns into soil, then it turns into food for the tree. In the autumn it loses all its leaves then the worm can draw down leaves so it turns into soil, then iit turns into food again for the tree, that soil..don't remember any more.

Fragments of the food chain

The children in this category have understood a few relations in the food chain, for example, that dead animals turn into food for the trees, that birds eat worms, etc.

Anna: The tree.... it lost its leaves, then they got new leaves.

Interviewer: What happened to the leaves when they reached the ground?

Anna: It turned into soil..

Kristina: Some animals died. The worms died of the birds almost...then they had a xxxxxx....(She uses a word here *störtlopp* that includes part of the Swedish word for cycle *kretslopp* but means downhill race.)

Interviewer: What is a xxxxxx?

Kristina: It's sort of... animals then different things happen, they maybe die like.

Cecilia: Birds eat worms.

Name parts

The children in this category name and point out parts that were included in the cycle or something else that they had notice, that is, they list them without relating them to each other.

Martin: He talked about animals.... birds.

Interviewer: Was there anything else he talked about?

Martin: Worms.

Interviewer: What happened to those animals then?

Martin: Don't know.

Camilla: They killed them or something .. then we saw a bear.

Marie: Yes, blackbird and fieldfare.

Interviewer: What happened to them?

Marie: It died.

Interviewer: Did he tell you anything else?

Marie: don't know.

Karin: We were allowed to look at the birds, then we were allowed to pat the wolf, and then a stuffed bear , too.. then we saw a dead bird too.

Interviewer: What happened to the animals... what happened to the dead bird?

Karin: (no reply).

Mathias: About a bird, and about the tree and about the wolf, no not the wolf.

Interviewer: Where there any other animals?

Mathias: Insects.

Interviewer: What happened to the animals?

Mathias: They were there... a plastic snake.. don't remember.

7.2.2 The number of answers in each category

We shall now see in Table 17 into what categories the children's answers in the different preschool groups are divided.

Table 17. Children's conceptions of the cycle

	Preschool			
	A	B	C	D
The cycle	10	8	1	2
The food chain	8	6	1	5
Fragments	1	2	6	9
Names of parts	-	3	10	1
No of children	19	19	18	17

The Chi^2 test shows that there is a significant difference between the experimental and control groups (X^2=17.4; $\underline{df}$=3;p=<.001). As the table also shows, more than half the children in group A have understood the cycle. The other children in this group (all but one) have understood the food chain. In the B group somewhat fewer children have understood both the cycle and the food chain. In group C only two children have understood the cycle or the food chain, while 7 children in group D have understand one of these. The co-judge's categories agreed with these for 89% of the children's answers.

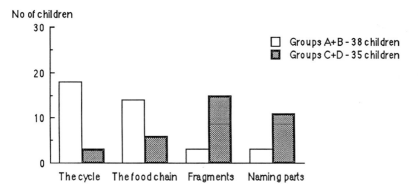

Figure 5. Block diagram illustrating how the experimental groups (A + B) and the control groups (C + D) understood the cycle.

As we can see in Figure 5, there is a marked difference between the experimental and the control groups. Working with the special didactic approach adopted in groups A and B appears to provide the children with a better foundation for understanding the cycle than, for example, children who worked with the content.

As mentioned earlier, those children who did not give any sign of understanding the cycle were given different parts from the cycle to use in a story. We can see in Table 18 how these children reason with the help of the concrete examples. This made the task considerably easier, of course. Many researchers believe that it is easier for children to retell stories if they have help from pictures (see, for example, Nurss and Hough, 1985).

Table 18. The story about the cycle using concrete material

	Preschool			
	A	B	C	D
The cycle	5	4	-	2
The food chain	3	5	5	9
Fragments	-	2	5	1
Naming parts	-	-	4	1
Making up a story	-	-	3	1
Don't know	-	-	1	-
No of answers	8(1)	11	17	15

This table includes only those children who did not express anything showing that they had understood the cycle. One child in group A was not given this task. With the help of the concrete material, a further quarter of the children in groups A and B show in their answers that they have understood the cycle. No child in group C appears to have been helped by the concrete material. All the children in group D now express an understanding of the food chain, but still only a few of them have any conception of the cycle.

To the interviewer's question "Do you remember what Kalle called it when he drew arrows between all the different parts?" the children replied, for example, the cycle, the master race, the downhill race, circle, race, etc. (See earlier explanation of the connection between the Swedish words used here.) It is obvious that numerous suggestions were made! To the question why Kalle drew arrows between the different parts, one child said: "Just so we would understand, he put them in a ring".

7.3 Discussion

Group A, who worked with the structure in the form of a cycle, is also the group that understood the ecological cycle to the greatest extent. If one examines the result as a whole, it is not, however, possible to relate these to working with specific structures. It seems rather that the deciding factor as to whether the children have understood the ecological cycle or not is the didactic approach adopted in their preschool programme.The didactic approach in group B was the same as in group A, but the relationship the children particularly noticed was that of cause and effect. Somewhat fewer children understood the cycle in group B than in group A, but in comparison with groups C and D, there were surprisingly many. In the latter groups only one or two children have understood the complete cycle, while a third of the children in group D have understood a relation in the form of a food chain. This group has worked with food chains previously, which, of course, may be seen as examples of a relationship similar to that of the cycle (except that they are not closed). With the help of concrete material, most of the children in group D also manage to talk about the food chain. It is difficult to understand why most of the children in group C only name or list the parts, or name fragments. It is even more puzzling in view of the fact that it was in this group, too, that the lesson at the museum was most clearly presented as regards the ecological cycle.

The conclusion that one can draw about the actual presentation of the learning experiment is that it does not appear to play any decisive role, since the "best" lesson produced the "worst" results and the "worst" teaching, in Group A where the teacher confused food chains and cycles, did not have the effect of making it more difficult for the children to understand the cycle but rather the opposite.

It is difficult to find any examples in the literature of studies of how preshool children understand cycles of the type examined here. On the other hand, there are studies of schoolchildren's ideas about, for example, the circulation in the body (Andersson, 1987) and about what happens to a corpse in the earth (Julin & Peterson, 1987). Birgersson (1988) has carried out a study of how schoolchildren (in Forms 3, 6 and 9) understand the life-cycle of the bean. She says that age, maturity, experience and school education all play a role in the developmnet of children's conceptions of ecological systems towards more and more abstract thinking.

PART 4. DISCUSSION

8. SUMMARY AND CONCLUSIONS

As pointed out earlier, the project "Meta-learning in the preschool" is a descriptive study designed similarly to an experiment insofar as the project leader introduced a certain way of working in groups A and B. It is is important to emphasise that the teachers in these two groups have only worked with <u>certain</u> aspects of preschool activities, and that only these have been the focus of this study. This means that if the preschools were compared in relation to any other aspect of the activities, the picture could be quite different. This also implies that the comparison between the groups should not be regarded as the complete "truth" but only in relation to my particular line of research, that is, developing children's conceptions about their own learning and certain forms of understanding about the world around them.Teachers A and B have, in other words, worked with trying to develop those things that preschool children have been shown in earlier studies to realise only to a minor extent, such as, for example, that they can learn to know, that thye can acquire knowledge by experience, that what they do in preschool has something to do with the real world outside, and that they can understand things if they can see relationships.

A considerable body of data has been collected, both with regard to interviews of children and to observations. This may, of course, largely be ascribed to the fact that four different groups were involved. However, I deemed it important to have several teachers participating in the project with different viewpoints and ways of working. The reason why I conducted so many interviews in connection with learning experiments was that I wanted the material to cover as wide a ground as possible and to vary in content. The reason why I made observations (and sometimes tape-recordings) over the whole year is mainly that I wanted to obtain as true a picture as possible of the activities the children took part in. Another advantage of taking part in the work continually throughout the school year is that the children accept you as an everyday figure and do not merely regard you as someone who turns up on special occasions.

As already mentioned, teacher A had already done some work previously with the type of didactic approach forming the basis of this year's study, which explains why the study proceeded in line with my intentions early on in the school year. Teacher B had a great deal of other work which competed with the intentions of the project, such as the extensive collaboration with school, preparation for courses and many other activities. This meant that nearly the whole of the first term passed before the work began to function according to the objectives we had set up. However, what is interesting is that, despite the different starting-points, a common form of didactics was developed, but as ought to be case, it was naturally put into practice in different ways in the two groups.

Getting children to reflect on content, structure and learning has not caused any problems in the groups, nor has drawing their attention to the metacognitive aspects, that is, getting them to reflect on how they think about these. The problem has, if anything, concerned the design - how to isolate a certain structure? This has been difficult, naturally because various aspects of relationship overlap. If you take the story "On the other side of the river" as an example, here the children are required to understand the relation between cause and effect in order to understand why they built a new bridge, but the story can also be seen in the form of the relation between the whole and the parts as prerequisites for each other. Another reason may be that the teachers, by being made aware of structures themselves, now also notice them and draw the children's attention to them in many different connections.

8.1 Children's learning and development

Here we shall examine the results in each group as a whole, that is, the pattern formed by all the parts.

<u>Group A</u>
In this group children's conceptions of <u>what</u> they learn changed to the extent that about three quarters of them comprehend that they have learned to know about something by the end of the preschool year. All these children have an idea about <u>how</u> they have learned to know by being involved in

certain activities and situations themselves. Two of these children also have an idea that they can learn by thinking something out. The majority of the children express in their statements that they have developed a qualitatively more advanced conception of their own learning during the preschool year. Their awareness of the learning aspect was also expressed in the the fact that most of them thought that they had to visit the museum to learn something.

With regard to what this group has learned from the various learning experiments, it may be seen that more than half the children retold most of the events in "The story about the red apple." Only a few children were only able to reproduce one or two events. When the children had to find a name for the story "On the other side of the river", nearly all of them gave it a title that linked up with the theme. Almost half the children focused on the point of the story by saying the people were mutually dependent, when they were allowed to tell what the story was about in their own words.This relationship became even more distinct when they had to answer the question why a new bridge was built. All but three children then answered that it was because they needed each other. The last learning experiment was conducted at the museum and involved an ecological cycle. This was perceived by about half the children in the group as a closed cycle, while nearly all the others perceived a relationship in the form of a food chain that was not closed. When these children were given concrete material to help them, however, most of them succeeded in completing the cycle. With regard to both their awareness of their own learning and what they had learned in the various learning experiments, the children in group A were far superior.

Group B
In this group about half the children develop a qualitatively more advanced conception of what they learn during the year in preschool. However, few of these children understand that they learn by actively acquiring experience. About two thirds of the children are also aware of the fact they had to visit the museum to learn about animals.

As far as what the children have learned from the various learning experiments is concerned, it was shown that about one third reproduced most of the events in "The story about the red apple", and as many again only a few events. As for "The other side of the river", most of the children's suggestions for a title are linked up with the mutual dependence.

Half the children state that they built a new bridge because they needed each other. Barely half the children express that they have understood the cycle during the teaching at the museum. Most of the other children have understood the food chain. With the help of concrete material, three more managed to express the cycle. In relation to the A group, the attempt to develop children's awareness of their own learning in the B group has not met with such success nor have the children learned so much from the various learning experiments. In comparison with the C and D groups, however, their achievement is impressive.

Group C

In this group no development can be discerned, either with regard to <u>what</u> they think they have learned or <u>how</u> this happens. About a quarter of the children appear to have understood that they had to go to the museum to learn, while the rest know or believe that it was to <u>look</u> at animals.

As regards retelling of "The story about the red apple," no child in the group reproduced nearly all of the events. The vast majority of the children reproduced one or 2-4 events, indicating that very few children have understood what the story was about. Nor did any child express that they had comprehended the mutual dependence in the story "On the other side of the river" used in the second learning experiment. Almost a third do not know what the story was about and the rest can retell one or two parts. To the question why they built a new bridge, however, about a third state that they needed each other. Nevertheless, half the children give the story an irrelevant title or cannot think of one at all. Only one child has understood the cycle at the visit to the museum and again only one the food chain. Most of them report fragments of, or give a name to something, they have seen. Not even after being helped by going through it with concrete examples, does any other child succeed in expressing that they had understood the cycle. Compared with the other control group, these childrn have not developed their awareness of their own learning or succeeded in learning from the learning experiments, with the exception of the story "The other side of the river".

Group D

In this group about a third of the children interviewed express that they have developed their conception of <u>what</u> they learn in preschool, but they all believe that they learn to know (how) because someone has told them, that is, they are passive receivers. Barely half the children appear to have understood that the visit to the museum was intended to teach them something.

When reproducing "The story about the red apple," only a few children show that they have understood most of the events. The vast majority reproduce 2-4 events. More children give an irrelevant title to the story "The other side of the river", or cannot think of one that is linked up with the theme, than those who succeed in this respect. No child takes up the mutual dependence when retelling this story. To the question why they built a new bridge, only two children refer to the people's dependence on each other. Again only two children show in their answers that they have understood the cycle when visiting the museum. Most express that they have understood fragments. Two more children indicate an understanding of the cycle and most of the others manage the food chain after being helped with concrete examples. In contrast to the other control group (C), some children in this group developed some awareness that they are learning. In the learning experiments, they have sometimes understood better, sometimes worse than the children in group C.

<u>When one compares all the groups,</u> a dividing line can be seen in all parts between the A and B groups, on the one hand, and the C and D groups, on the other,with regard to awareness of their own learning and what they have actually learned. It is the children in the A group who have learned and developed most in all respects. In the C group no development of the children's awareness of their own learning takes place. In one of the learning experiments, a few children have indicated in their statements that they have understood the content of what they have been taught. In the D group some slight development (a few children) takes place as regards the conceptions of whatt they have learned. In the learning experiments there are generally a few childen who reach a more advanced level. The inter-judge reliability, that is, the number of categorised answers that were in agreement, varies between 78 and 93% in the various learning experiments and in respect of children's conceptions of learning.

8.2 The teachers' performance

<u>Teachers A och B</u>
The outlook and way of working introduced into groups A and B are based on the perspective of children and are characterised by a certain didactic approach. Children understand various phenomena in the world around them in different ways. Learning is a question of mental development, that is, of qualitatively understanding more aspects of the world around one than before (Doverborg, Qvarsell & Pramling, 1987). The teacher's role is to set up <u>goals in the form of various types of insight,</u> after which she has to provide the children with the opportunity to develop them. When a teacher has formulated these goals, the next step is to <u>find out the ways children think about them</u> in order to <u>create situations</u> in which children can be active both as regards thinking and acting (Doverborg & Pramling, 1988). What is in focus is the children's own activity and reflections but the teacher's guidance towards certain goals in the form of various phenomena. This means that attention is paid to <u>the structure of the understanding of the content.</u> Use is made of children's play and everyday situations to get them to think. Advantage is taken of the dynamics in the group (usually organised into small sub-groups) by drawing attention to the <u>different</u> ways children think. Children's mental development is not expected to occur as a result of the teacher imparting knowledge or of the children assimilating that which they are ripe for, but it involves an interaction between both between the children themselves and between the children and the teacher. As partners in the learning process, children are probably an untapped resource (see, for example, Damond, 1984; Frönes, 1985). Strömquist (1988) claims, for example, that there is no evidence that conversations with teachers always develop children's language more than those with peers. It is likely that children's thinking is developed in the same way, in interaction with other children as well as with the teacher.

Instead of a lesson in the A and B groups starting with a concrete experience, it often starts with the children having to think something out. An example of this is when the children in the A group talked about clouds. Instead of studying clouds, the children were urged by the teacher to reflect and draw what they think the clouds typical of fair, rainy or thundery weather look like. When all have formed an idea of these, they are studied in real life so as to be able to make comparisons both between the drawings of the children and between these and the real thing. The teachers in the A and

B groups quite simply rely on the children having an idea or conception, which they nearly always do! You can see this, for example, in the project "Solving problems by means of dialogues," which is based on the idea that all children first form a picture of how a problem should be solved before all the different solutions are illustrated and discussed with the teacher and the whole class (Easley & Stake, 1984). Corsaro (1985) also shows in his studies how that even at the age of four children are aware of social status, which comes out clearly in how they act in role plays, that is, they have understood and developed an idea about this to the effect, for example, that children taking the part of "children" in the role play never have any say in what "the father" should do. The alternative way of working in the A and B groups described here is an attempt to develop a preschool working method based on the research conducted within the school of phenomenography.

The performance of teachers A and B should be regarded as a didactic principle beginning in the abstract, that is, on the basis of children's experience. This principle can be compared with Davydov's theoretical generalisation (Hedegaard, 1988), which is based on the didactics in scientific concepts (as opposed to induction). A third didactic variant is that based on concrete material.

Teacher C

Both the words and actions of teacher C can be seen to express a view of maturity that was introduced into the preschool after the theories of Gesell and Ilgs (1961) became known in Sweden at the end of the forties and fifties. These theories can be regarded as a reaction against the authoritarian method of bringing up children that was usual in former days. These researchers observed both the "natural" daily rhythm of children and what was characteristic of child development at different ages, that is, of what children usually do and how they usually do it at different events of development. They were interested in how a democratic individual could be formed in society.They thought that the teacher should adapt herself to the child and neither force the child to do anything nor force knowledge onto them. The teacher should be actively passive, meaning that she should be observant regarding the child's needs and supply material so that the child itself is able to go on developing. These theories took up many different aspects of child development in that they dealt with motor, emotional, social and intellectual development. Teacher C appears to be an ideal teacher according to the theory of maturity. She is actively passive both in the class sessions when she largely allows children's own associations to predominate, and also when she steps in with support or help when they ask for it. When she asks them about things in the class session, this is also usually to give someone a chance to show that he/she knows something and to tell the rest about it. There is very little traditional teaching. What the children learn, they learn by <u>actively doing.</u> This is a hypothesis that is apparent in teacher C's work and that can also be attributed to a Piagetian, constructivist viewpoint.

<u>Teacher D</u>
In her teaching teacher D has definite goals relating to knowledge, which can partly be compared with those of school, that is, a subject or an area is taken up and the teacher painstakingly covers all the aspects she thinks are relevant. The class session very much resembles a lesson in which the teacher attempts to <u>impart</u> something. The exercises in connection with different areas are also planned by the teacher in such a way that what the children do leads to an end-product similar to her own. This even applies in periods for freer creativity, that is, there is a model or pattern for the children to follow. When, occasionally, this is not available, some children display uncertainty. In her interview, the teacher herself points out that she focuses more on learning these days than earlier. It is obvious that learning is related to school knowledge that the children are expected to <u>acquire</u> if they listen to teacher and then consolidate in various types of exercises. First you talk, then you work with it in some active fashion. As far as the children's creativity is concerned, the prevailing tradition is that of Fröbel, with models and prototypes. Perhaps one can say that this is a question of a modern version of the infant schools, in which interest has revived in Sweden today. Most characteristic of the infant schools are the organisation and the structure, consisting of lessons and exercises that everyone has to participate in, over and over again, until everyone has mastered them. Johansson's (1987) research into the structure of class sessions (in the form of how the teacher succeeds in conducting them according to his plan) to explain the more general behaviour of children in the child groups (in play and solving conflicts) lends support to this type of preschool programme. (For this didactic approach, see also Sundell, 1988).

8.2.1 Comparisons

The two views of preschool activities exhibited by teachers C and D are both common. Doverborg (1987), for example, has described the different ideas teachers have about preparation for arithmetic. She found that some teachers believe that children should be taught about figures, number and ordinals, etc., by taking these up and talking about them (and doing exercises) for a limited amount of time, that is, as a theme. The children acquire knowledge through the teacher who supplies it. Other teachers think that you need do nothing, since arithmetical aspects form a natural part of preschool activities. They refer to counting children, looking at the calendar, laying the table, etc., every day, and in this way, the children obtain an arithmetical basis, that is, they realise this when they are mature enough. The same view of maturity underlies the third viewpoint described by Doverborg, but its effect on the work is another. These teachers believe that children are not ready for arithmetic and that it is therefore no concern of the preschool.

To rely only on children assimilating what is available in their environment and not to try to supply them with facts but to actively and purposefully direct their attention and reflections towards certain aspects of the world around them, as teachers A and B do, is not a particularly widespread method of working in preschool, even though preschool teachers often find these ideas attractive. As early as the end of the forties, Sandels (1949) wrote that preschool staff had much to learn from Piaget's research into children's thinking. At the beginning of the seventies, it was the Committee on Child Day Care Centres who highlighted Piaget's research again. This placed the child in the centre, that is, the child with its subjective world, from which knowledge was then constructed. It was certainly good that Piaget's research was given its due and that the child's world was taken seriously, but this is not enough as far as education is concerned. Teachers A and B have partly worked according to its interactive theories, which the Committee on Child Day Care Centres introduced, but they have also had a well-defined focus in combination with a metacognitive level, which they have brought out.

It would be possible to claim that this study deals with case studies, that is, individual teachers are examined. It would be equally possible to claim that they represent different established perspectives, both within learning research and educational practice. In group D, it is the teacher's performance that is important, that is, what she is capable of giving the children. Here the content is obvious and of significance. In contrast to this, the teacher of C group can be seen as completely child-centred, that is, it is the children's spontaneous interest that is the decisive factor. According to the teacher herself, children construct the knowledge that they are ready for. In this way, the content fades into the background, just as it did in the Committee on Child Day Care Centres. The teachers in groups A and B have tried to develop a third way, which implies that it is children's thinking about the content that is the point of departure. Children's perspective has a prominent place, but in combination with a deliberate choice of content on the part of the teacher.

Marton and Neuman (1988) have described the difference between constructivism and the viewpoint on which this study is based, which they designate constitutionalism. According to constructivism, the child creates its own world, which is a subjective world that differs and is separate from the concrete reality that is available to them. According to the ideas of constitutionalism, which emanate from "the phenomenological movement", the child and the world form a unit, that is, the child lives in a world, a world that is comprehended and experienced as a thought about the world. This world is both objective and subjective, a reality that is the only one we have.

In what sense then have the children had a comparable preschool year? In all groups they had a busy year with themes and activities connected with the three areas: nature, culture and society (The Board of Health and Welfare, 1987). The areas associated with content have involved different structures (in the form of relationships). However, special attention has been drawn to these only in groups A and B, by getting children to reflect on relationships regarding the different contents they have worked with. Naturally, the children in all the groups have been questioned from time to time in order to find out what they are thinking, but the metacognitive level of children's reflections on the learning aspect and how they think about this and other content-related aspects has only been brought out in groups A and B. Moreover, only in the experimental groups has teaching alternated between different levels of generality.

8.3 Educational implications

There are a number of studies within the sphere of higher education that follow similar lines to the one reported here (see, for example, Biggs, 1986; Martin & Ramsten, 1987). The studies that I have found that deal with children at a lower age level are both Danish and are clearly influenced by Russian educationists.

Hedegaard (1988) has carried out an interesting teaching experiment during one school year in a fourth form in school. The background of this teaching experiment may be found in the Russian school forms. Vygotsky's zone concept (Vygotsky, 1972) in particular, is used, and also Davydov's didactic instructions with conceptual generalizations. The teaching experiment begins with the children being asked to draw what they could investigate if they were scientists and, in the next stage, what they could investigate in general science. Here the teacher has guided the children's thoughts both towards <u>how</u> you can acquire knowledge and <u>what</u> the content of general science is to the children.

The teacher starts out from a theoretical model about the development of animal species and how they change in relation to nature. With the children, however, the teacher only takes up one aspect at a time, such as, for example, what effect some natural change has on the variation of a species, what importance climate has, what animals live in the artic and what live in the tropics, what animals eat and their relation to nature, etc., to finally concentrate on the variation in the offspring and the survival of animals when nature has changed, as well as how the variation in their way of life can be be changed so that new species arise.

The teacher hold dialogues with the class throughout the year, that is, conversations that are directed towards the problem areas from the model. Teaching goes from the content of the subject (for the children) to what it means to be a scientist. The next stage is to give the children new experience that can be worked on and made the subject of reflection. They draw conclusions and focus on relationships and connections in the model, to throw light once again on the scientist and the new questions he asks. Now and again they summarise what they have arrived at on the basis of the goals that have been set up. Particular animals are studied and related to the list of categories. Once again the focus is on <u>what</u> they are studying, and so it goes on towards a reality of growing complexity.

The teacher draws up plans on the basis of the general laws in the real world around us with all its complexity. The children's learning moves from that based on experience and action to symbolisation of the insight they gain through their exploration, which results in linguistic formulations of relationships.

Hedegaard (op cit) says that observations show that the motive develops from the point where children are interested in doing research like scientists and show an interest in prehistoric animals, fossils and animals on Greenland to an interest in the stages of scientific work connected with formulating questions, reviewing what they know and compiling lists of what they do not know. After this the interest in animals develops into an interest in understanding animals in a general context, as covered by the model, and an interest in discussing what the consequences would be if anything in the model were changed (e.g. the climate).

Both in Hedegaard's study and the one reported here the content of teaching concerns problems of understanding, that is, problems that require the children to see relationships in order to understand. To be sure, Hedegaard works with more complex relationships, since her children are considerably older than the preschool children in this study. Nevertheless, one cay say that Hedegaard's teaching experiment alternates between reflections on a content and reflections on the content in relation to the structure (which consists of a model), while getting children to reflect from time to time on how they learn (starting off from the work of the scientist). Another similarity between the studies is the teachers' purposeful guidance towards relationships by directing the work on children's reflections towards these, while the children work in a concrete fashion on the basis of their experience.

Broström (1988) is yet another educationist who has been inspired by Vygotsky and other Russian researchers. In his work with developing forms of activity and educational principles for 6-year-olds, Broström is of the opinion that the content should be selected on the basis of educational considerations, while the form of activity (the way of working) should be decided on the basis of psychological considerations. He also thinks that the task of the teacher is to create conditions in which the child is able to gain experience of various fundamental phenomena, but that it is the child's own activity that makes it try to obtain a result. The principles he assumes are that children assimilate "the world" through play and that development moves from the visual (perception) to experience by use of models such as general principles. The further the model is from reality, the closer it is to being symbolic and the further the child has come to acquiring logical experience, says Broström. He also thinks that the child concentrates first on the product and then becomes aware of the process. Here there are clear parallels with Piaget, who believes that the results precede an awareness of how the result has been obtained (Piaget, 1976; 1978).

Broström (op cit) describes three themes that are carried out with the 6-year-olds. One, "A week in the wood", aims at bringing out the essence of nature (that it is living) and drawing attention to relationships. The second theme "Three weeks with iron" (things) is the antithesis of nature, but also brings out a relationship in the form of cause - effect (what happens to iron when it is heated?). The third theme deals with "Symbols", as a basis for learning to read and write. The teacher tells the children they are going to learn a new word, "symbol". She explains this as "it's something you put instead of something else". The children's reflections take over and someone draws symbols from the orienteering maps. They realise that their drawings are instead of real things, that the bank-notes they have made for the shop game take the place of real money, that David stands for the boy David, etc. Eventually they begin to make various road signs and talk about letters of the alphabet. On other occasions the teacher creates situations in which the children have to sing or act according to symbols.

The teachers in Broström's study work deliberately towards getting the children to understand certain phenomena or aspects of reality by letting them ponder about them. On several occasions the teacher also asks: "What should you do to find out...?", that is, she tries to get the children to reflect on their own learning. This aspect is not, however, brought out in a specially systematic manner. Broström's study is also very similar to the one reported here, in that the focus is on various phenomena in the children's world and on getting them to reflect on these on the basis of situations the teacher has created. Where they differ is in respect of the metacognitive level. Here they do not draw the children's attention to how they think about it. They only hint incidentally that they draw the children's attention to how they learn, but never to how they think about it. Nor is there any direct evaluation in Broström's study of whether the children have developed understanding, and if so what, during the year in the kindergarten.

To take the children's way of thinking as the point of departure is not only an educational approach, but has, of course, psychological significance. Bae (1988) thinks that the quality of the relations between children and teacher creates conditions for what children learn, both regard to content and about themsleves.

To be acknowledged as children on their own terms, that is, on the basis of their way of thinking, in whatever way they think, has a decisive influence on children's will and motivation for reflecting further. Far too often, we teachers supply the children with preconceived ideas instead of attending to and reflecting their own ideas, says Bae. She thinks that, by being acknowledged, children are given the opportunity to draw positive conclusions about their own world. This is an experience that has a strong bearing on continued learning.

By taking the children's world seriously, one creates the necessary conditions for children to learn and gain confidence in their own ability. Helping children to learn ought to be the most important task of the preschool. This is not, however, anything that children do automatically through their imagination and play being given free rein. Nor do children learn by being forced to concentrate on or listen to facts which somebody tries to transmit to them. Helping children to learn is a question of getting them to understand certain aspects of reality by thinking.

In the U.S.A. there is a great interest in developing "effective thinking". Kuhn (1987) says that most programmes are aimed at teaching children principles and rules for thinking. She claims, however, that the most effective way of developing thinking is to involve children in thinking.

Schickedaz (1982) says that when you, for example, teach children to read, this is done in the form of teaching isolated skills in a predetermined sequence (see also Smith, 1986). This procedure is based on the idea that reading must be simplified if children are to understand it, and that learning is chiefly linear, that is, a question of gradually building up associations until everything forms a whole.This is contradicted by the fact that some children learn to read themselves without anything being simplified. Schickedaz believes that these children have had access to experience of a sufficiently complex nature to provide them with fundamental knowledge of the reading process. To support children's learning, you can add things to simplify the situation without necessarily destroying the content. She gives the following examples: you can help a child to learn to cycle by fixing support wheels to the bicycle, teach small children to draw by giving them thicker crayons that are easier to hold, help children to browse through a story book by having thicker pages, etc. The child thus gets help with dealing with situations without essential knowledge being destroyed.

In the same way, we in the preschool should focus on various phenomena in the children's world as a whole, instead of trying to teach children on the basis of small, isolated elements. To simplify without destroying the complexity of the various phenomena can often be done by working with analogies, that is, concrete situations illustrating phenomena of various kinds. But it is not enough to supply concrete illustrations; it is far more important to help children to reflect on the reality, the structures and themselves.

By requiring the children in this study to reflect, largely in play and in situations of an everyday nature or created by the teacher, the children have not only become aware of <u>how</u> they learn, but have also become <u>better at learning a new content.</u> In other words, there is a relationship between the child's metacognitive capacity and the possibility of learning, which can be developed by applying the didactics from the study groups described here.

References

Andersson, B. (1987). Elevers begrepp om människokroppen - en översikt. (Pupils' conceptions of the human body.) Institutionen för pedagogik, Göteborgs universitet.

Brown, A. (1985). Teaching students to think as they read: Implications for curriculum reform. Paper presented at the American Educational Research Association. Washington,D.C.

Brown, A. & Reeve, R. (1985). Metacognition Reconsidered: Implications for Intervention Research. Journal of Abnormal Child Psychology. 13 (3), 343-356.

Bae, B. (1988). Voksnes definisjonsmakt og barns selvopplevelse. (Adults' power of definition and children's self-awareness.) Norsk Pedagogisk Tidskrift. 4.

Berstein, B. (1971). Class, codes and control. Vol 1. Theoretical studies towards a sociology of language. London: Routledge & Kegan, Paul.

Biggs, J. (1986). Enhancing learning skills: The role of meta-cognition. I J.A. Bowden. (Ed) Student learning: Research into practice. Centre for the study of higher education.

Birgersson, E. (1988). Elevers bergeppsuppfattning och tankar om bönans livscykel. (Children's conceptions of and thoughts about the life-cycle of the bean.) Överbryggande kurs i Na-pedagogik, Göteborgs universitet.

Broström, S. (1988). Udvikling af virksomhedsformer og peadagogiske principper for de 6 årige. (Developmnet of forms of activity and educational principles for six-year-olds.) (Manuscript)

Corsaro, W. (1985). Friendship and Peer Culture in Early Years. New York: Ablex.

Dahlgren, G. & Olsson, L.E. (1985). Läsning i barnperspektiv. (Reading from the point of view of the child.) Göteborg: Acta Universitatis Gothoburgensis.

Dahlberg, G. (1985). Context and the Children's Orientation to Meaning. Malmö: Liber Förlag.

Damond, W. (1984). Peer Education. The untapped potential. Journal of applied developmental psychology, 5, 331-343.

Doverborg, E., & Pramling, I. (1985). Att förstå barns tankar - metodik för barnintervjuer. (Understanding children's thoughts - methodology for interviewing children.) Stockholm: Liber.

Doverborg, E. (1987). Matematik i förskolan? (Mathematics in preschool?) Publikation nr 5. Institutionen för pedagogik. Göteborgs universitet.

Doverborg, E. & Johansson, J-E. (1986). Förskolans pedagogik - historik, dagsläge och plats i lärareutbildningen. (Educational methods in the preschool - historical background, present situation and place in teacher training.) In Marton (Ed), Fackdidaktik vol 1, 173-190, Lund: Studentlitteratur.

Doverborg, E. & Pramling, I. (1987). I dag var det verkligen bra problem vi fick! (We got a really good thing to puzzle out today!) Förskolan.2.

Doverborg, E., Pramling, I.& Qvarsell, B. (1987). Inlärning och utveckling. (Learning and development.) Stockholm: Utbildningsförlaget.

Doverborg, E. & Pramling, I. (1988). Temaarbete. Lärarens metodik och barns förståelse. (Working with a theme. Teaching methods and children's understanding.) Stockholm: Utbildningsförlaget.

Dayson, A. (1982). The Emergence of Visible Language: Interrelationship between Drawing and Early Writing. Visible Language. XVI, 4, 360-381.

Easley, J, Stake, B. (1984). Development and evaluation of dialogic teacher education in primary mathematics and science problem solving. College of Education, University of Urbana-Champagne.

Francis, H. (1982). Learning to read. London: George Allen & Unwin.

Flavell, J. (1979). Metacognition and Cognitive Monitoring. American Psychologist, 34.

Frönes, I. (1985). Jämnåriga som läromästare. (Peers as teachers.) In L.E. Lundmark & K. Stridsman. (Ed). Sen kommer en annan tid. En antiologi om barns och ungdoms livsformer. Stockholm: Liber/Allmänna Förlaget.

Gesell, A. & Ilg, F. (1961). Barnets värld och vår. (Infants and Children in the Culture of Today). Stockholm: Natur och Kultur.

Goodnow, J. (1985). Children's Drawing. London: Fontana Press.

Hedegaard, M. (1988). Skolebörns personlighedsudvikling set genom orienteringsfagene (Personality development of children seen through general science subjects.) Århus: Universitetsförlaget.

Hundeide, K. (1987). Barns livsvärlden. (A child's experience of the world) (manuscript).

Hamilton, M. (1986). Knowledge and communication in children. I C. Antaki & A. Lewis (Eds). Mental Mirrors. London: SAGE Publications.

Johansson, B. (1987). Conventional and moral rules in the pre-school context. Contribution presented at NFPF:s conference in Copenhagen 19-22 March.

Julin, U. & Peterson, E. (1986). Barns tankar om döden. (Children's thoughts about death).

Kroksmark, T. (1987). Fenomenografisk didaktik. (Phenomenographic didactics.) Göteborg: Acta Universitatis Gothoburgensis.

Kuhn, D. (1987). Education for thinking. Invited address given at the conference "Thinking and Problemsolving in the Developmental Process: International Perspectives. Rutgers University, April 10-12.

Lybeck, L. (1981). Arkimedes i klassen. (Archimedes in the classroom.) Göteborg: Acta Universitatis Gothoburgensis.

Larsson, S. (1986). Kvalitativ analys.(Qualitative analysis.) Lund: Studentlitteratur.

Lööf,U. (1974). Sagan om det röda äpplet. (The story about the red apple.)

Martin, F. & Ramsten, P. (1987). Learning skills, or skill in learning. In I.T.E. Richardson, M.W. Eysench & D.W. Piper (Eds). Student learning. Milton Keynes: Open University Press. pp 155-169.

Marton, F. (1981). Phenomenography - discribing conceptions of the world around us. Instructional Science. Vol.10, 177-200.

Marton, F. (1986) Some reflections on the improvement of learning. I J.A. Bowden (Ed). Student learning: Research into practice. Centre for the study og Higher Education. Melbourne University.

Marton, F. (1988). Revealing educationally critical differences in our understanding of the world around us. Paper presented at the American Educational Research Association. New Orleans.

Marton, F. & Neuman, D. (1988). Constructivism versus constitutionalism. Some implications for the first mathematics education. Paper presented at the Sixth International Congress on Mathematical Education, July 27-August 3.

Murray, F. (1987). Neo-Piagetian research. Lecture at the Northeastern Educational Research Association, Ellenville 28-30 Okt.

Merleay-Ponty, M. (1962). Phenomenology of Perception. London: Routledge & Kegan.

Neuman, D. (1987). The origin of arithmetic skills. Göteborg: Acta Universitatis Gothuborgensis.

Nurss, J. & Hough, R. (1985). Young children's oral language: Effects of Task. Journal of Educational Research, 78, (5).

Oppenheim, J. (1987). På andra sidan ån. (On the other side of the river.) Stockholm: Litteraturfrämjandet.

Piaget, J. (1970). The child's conception of physical causality. London: Routledge & Kegan.

Piaget, J. (1975). The child's conception of the world. New Jersey: Litterfield, Adams & Co. (original 1929).

Piaget, J. (1976). The grasp of consciousness.Cambridge Mass.: Harward University Press.

Piaget, J. (1978). Success and understanding. London: Routledge & Kegan Paul.

Pramling, I. (1983a). The child's conception of learning. Göteborg: Acta Universitatis Gothoburgensis.

Pramling, I. (1983b). Möte med arbetslivet. (A meeting with the working life.) Rapport från Pedagogiska institutionen, Göteborgs universitet. Nr. 1.

Pramling, I. (1987a). Att arbeta med skolkunskapens osynliga grund. (Working with the invisible foundations of school knowledge.) Bidrag presenterat på NFPF:s konferens i Köpenhamn 19-22 mars.

Pramling, I. (1986a). Barn och inlärning. (Children and learning.) Lund: Studentlitteratur.

Pramling, I. (1986b). Meta-inlärning i förskolan. Förskolebarns uppfattningar av inlärning och innehållet i temat "Affären". (Meta-learning in preschool. Preschool children's conpetions of learning and the content of the theme "The shop".) Publikation från Institutionen för pedagogik. Göteborgs universitet. Nr.15

116

Pramling, I. (1987b). Vad är metakognition?.(What is metacognition?) Publikation från Institutionen för pedagogik, Göteborgs universitet. Nr. 07.

Pramling, I. (1987c). Meta-inlärning i förskolan. En fenomengrafisk studie. (Meta-learning in preschool. A phenomenographic study.) Publikation från Institutionen för pedagogik, Göteborgs universitet. Nr. 09.

Pramling, I. (1987d). Att se världen genom barns ögon. (Seeing the world through the eyes of children.) Bidrag presenterat på symposiet "Barnintervjun som forskningsmetod". Uppsala 10-11 sept.

Pramling, I. (1988a). Att utveckla förskolebarns uppfattningar av några samhälleliga aspekter. (Developing preschool children's concepts of some aspects of society.) Bidrag presenterat på NFPF:s konferens i Oslo 10-13 mars.

Pramling, I. (1988b). Developing childrens thinking of their own learning. British Journal of Educational Psychology.58, 266-278.

Qvarsell, B. (1988). Barn, kultur och inlärning. (Children, culture and learning.) Stockholm: Centrum för kulturforskning.

Rasmussen, J. (1988). Å laere å laere. (Learning to learn) Kristiansand: Universitetsforlaget AS.

Sandels, S. (1949). Piaget och en del av hans verk. (Piaget and some of his work). Barnträdgården. Nr. 7.

Schickedaz, J. (1982). The acquisition of written Language in young children. I B. Spodek (Ed). Handbook of Research in Early Childhood Education. New York: The Free Press.

SOU 1972:26, 27. Förskolan 1, 2. (The Preschool, 1.2).

SOU 1985:22. Förskola -skola. (Preschool-school).

Socialstyrelsen (1987).Pedagogiskt program för förskolan. (Educational programme for preschools.) Stockholm: Liber.

Smith, F. (1986). Insult to intelligence. New York: Arbor House.

Småbarns-Skolor. (Infants schools.) (1837). Skrifter no 1. Utgifne af sällskapet för inrättande af Småbarns-skolor. Johan Högbergs Tryckeri.

Strömqvist, G. (1988). Samtal som arbetsform, några undervisningsmetodiska synpunkter. (Dialogues as a way of working, some views on teaching methods.) In S. Strömqvist & G. Strömqvist.

Samtal som arbetsform. Vad, hur, varför, skrifter från Institutionen för metodik i lärarutbildningen, Göteborgs universitet. Nr. 1.

Sundell, K. (1988). Day Care and Children's Development. Uppsala: Acta Universitatis Upsaliensis.

Säljö, R. (1982). Learning and understanding. Göteborg: Acta Universitatis Gothoburgensis.

Zirinsky, S. (1985). Children's Levels of Comprehension of Stories and Application of their Thematic Structure. Dept of Ed. London University.

Vygotsky, L.S. (1972). Taenkning og språg l og ll. (Thinking and language I and II.) Copenhagen: Mezhdunarodnaja Kinga og Hans Reitzels Forlag A/S.(original published in 1956).

Appendix 1

DISTRIBUTION OF 5 AND 6-YEAR-OLDS IN GROUPS C AND D

Some of the most important tables from different parts of the study.

Table 5. Children's ideas about what they had learnt in preschool just after
the start and at the end of the school year (5/6 years)

| | Preschool | | | |
| | C | | D | |
Occasion	1	2	1	2
To do	5/10	6/10	4/10	3/7
To know	-/1	-/1	1/-	3/2
To understand	-/-	-/-	-/-	-/-
Don't know	1/1	-/3	1/2	-/-
No of children	6/12	6/14	6/12	6/9

Table 7. Children's conceptions of how they learnt to do something (5/6
years)

| | Preschool | | | |
| | C | | D | |
Occasion	1	2	1	2
By doing	3/8	6/8	2/5	3/5
By being told or shown	1/2	-/2	3/5	-/2
By thinking things out	1/-	-/-	-/-	-/-
No of children	6/12	6/14	6/12	6/9

Table 8. <u>Children's conceptions of how they have learnt to know</u>

	Preschool			
	C		D	
Occasion	1	2	1	2
External influence	-/1	-/1	-/1	3/4
Own activity	-/-	-/-	-/-	-/-
Thinking	-/-	-/-	-/-	-/-
No of children	-/1	-/1	-/1	3/2

Table 10. <u>"The story about the red apple" - the number of events that were</u> <u>retold.</u>

	Preschool	
	C	D
8 - 11 events	-/-	1/2
5- 7 events	2/3	-/1
2 - 4 events	1/7	5/7
1 event	3/3	1/-
No of children	6/13	6/11

Table 13. <u>What children say spontaneously about the plot of the story "The</u> <u>other side of the river".</u>

	Preschool	
	C	D
Mutual dependence	-/-	-/-
One section	5/9	5/7
Don't know	1/5	1/4
No of children	6/14	6/11

Table 15. <u>Children's conceptions of why a new bridge was built</u>

	Preschool	
	C	D
Needed each other	1/6	-/2
To get across	2/2	3/3
Became friends	1/1	-/5
Don't know	2/5	3/1
No of children	6/14	6/11

Table 17. <u>Children's ideas about the ecological cycle</u>

	Preschool	
	C	D
The cycle	-/1	-/2
The food chain	-/1	1/4
Fragments	1/5	4/5
Naming parts	4/6	1/-
No of children	5/13	6/11

Index